Reading the Gospel

Reading the Gospel

John S. Dunne

University of Notre Dame Press

NOTRE DAME, INDIANA

Library of Congress Cataloging-in-Publication Data

Dunne, John S., 1929–
Reading the Gospel / John S. Dunne.
     p.   cm.
   Includes bibliographical references and index.
   ISBN 0-268-01667-4 (cloth : alk. paper) — ISBN 0-268-01668-2
(paper : alk. paper)
   1. Bible N.T. Gospels—Reading.   I. Title.
BS2555.5 .D865 2000
226'.06—dc21
                                                00-023572

CONTENTS

PREFACE

Reading for Writing,[1] that is the title of a textbook I read many years ago when I went to college, and that is what I am doing here, I realize now, reading for writing. I am reading the Gospel for writing this book and also for composing words and music, the Songlines of the Gospel at the end of this book. Reading for writing is in some ways akin to the ancient way of reading, reading aloud or even singing, as when reciting the Koran. It has that intermediate moment of silence, though, that comes of reading silently, and that silence is essential for the writing and the composing.

"We all have within us a center of stillness surrounded by silence,"[2] Dag Hammarskjöld says, beginning his little handout for the Meditation Room at the United Nations. Reading the Gospel leads us into that inner silence, and that is the essential method I want to use here, *lectio divina,* "divine reading," letting the words speak to the heart. So there are essentially three phases in reading. First of all there is the word we read, "In the beginning was the Word." Then there is the inner silence of the heart, taking the word to heart and letting it speak to the heart. And then there is the word we write or compose, as if to say "In the end was the Word." I think of Hermann Broch's novel *The Death of Virgil* and how it ends with the sentence "it was the word beyond speech,"[3] as if to end as the Gospel of John begins, with the eternal Word.

Indeed, if there is an answer to death, it is "the word beyond speech," and it seems that is the answer we find in the gospel, "And the light shines in the darkness, and the darkness has not overshadowed it."

Although it is "the word beyond speech," it becomes flesh, according to the gospel, it becomes accessible to us, speaking to us "the words of eternal life." What then is the answer to death? "In place of death there was light,"[4] as Tolstoy says in *The Death of Ivan Ilych*. There are three great metaphors in the Gospel of John, life and light and love, and they are metaphors of an abundant life, of a divine abundance. If we put these metaphors side by side with the parables of Matthew and Mark and Luke, we come to an idea that "grace is infinite,"[5] as Isak Dinesen says in "Babette's Feast," that the road taken in life rejoins the road not taken and ultimately there is one road, a road that does not dead-end but goes ever on, what mystics call "the road of the union of love with God."

Or so I read the Gospel. Thus understood the Gospel is indeed "good news." But what of other ways of reading it? There is *The Quest of the Historical Jesus* of which Albert Schweitzer wrote, and there is its continuance into our own times. Yet our relation with Jesus, as I understand it, is not a relation with a figure of the past but with a figure of the present. We enter into his relation with God, the God he calls Abba, hallowing the name, awaiting the kingdom, seeking the will of God, asking for the bread of heaven, forgiving and being forgiven, asking to be guided and guarded from temptation and evil. And so for us Jesus is alive and lives in our hearts. It is a matter of entering into his relationship with God, letting his God be our God, letting his *thou* become our *thou* and his *I am* become our own *I am* so he can say "I in them and thou in me." He disappears, then, from in front of us, and we find ourselves in his relation with God, but he is dwelling in us and we in him.

All the same, it is possible to read in quest of the historical Jesus. But it is important, it seems to me, to let this be a quest of understanding rather than a quest of certainty. For there is something self-defeating about the quest of certainty: the more intensely we seek certainty the more uncertain we become. And that is the reason, I believe, for the "negative result"[6] that Schweitzer found in the quest. If instead we seek understanding, the quest becomes compatible with a reading in "faith seeking understanding" (*fides quarens intellectum*), the kind of reading I am trying to do here.

"Song is the leap of mind in the eternal breaking out into sound,"[7] and that leap is the one I am trying to make at the end in Songlines of the Gospel. I take the title from *The Songlines* of Bruce Chatwin, where he traces the songlines running across aboriginal Australia, geographical lines going thousands of miles, each with its own guiding song. I thought to write guiding songs based on the Gospel, a kind of lyrical commentary on the Gospel of John. You learn something about words when you set them to music. And I find I have learned something about the Gospel in the songlines I have composed. I have become very aware of my own "leap of mind" as well as of "the eternal breaking out into sound."

On Reading

We read to know that we are not alone.
—Shadowlands

"We read to know that we are not alone,"[1] it is said in *Shadowlands,* the screenplay about C. S. Lewis, for reading, as Proust says, is "that fertile miracle of a communication effected in solitude."[2] What happens when we read, or what can happen, I believe, is that we *pass over* into other lives and times, and then we *come back* to our own life and times. That is what happens also when we read the Gospel, for "heart speaks to heart" as we read of the good tidings of "God with us," Emmanuel, then bring the good news back to our own life and times, and so it is indeed a way of knowing we are not alone.

I think of the stories I read as a child and of the stories I read now, for instance the Merlin trilogy by Mary Stewart[3], and how I find words there that speak to my heart: "to be alone in the secret dark, where a man is his own master, except for death" (p. 21), "the gods only go with you if you put yourself in their path" (p. 52), "What I would do and where I would go, I had no idea, but the god had sent me . . . and I trusted my fate" (p. 86), "Once I got my bearings, no doubt the god would lead me" (p. 88), "truth is the shadow of God" (pp. 135–36), "the gods do not visit you to remind

1

you of what you know already" (p. 223), "the gods do not speak to those who have no time to listen" (p. 238), "I had been so used to God's voice in the fire and the stars that I had forgotten to listen for it in the counsels of men" (p. 387), ". . . and who writes among the stars but God?" (p. 394), "It's never a wise thing to help kings to their heart's desire" (p. 394), "Then you must think it's worth it, life without women?—For me, yes—Well, then, come this way to your cold bed" (p. 396), "I have learned to look close at most things that come my way" (p. 436), "I had told myself only yesterday to look low as well as high for the things of power" (p. 484), "Every life has a death, and every light has a shadow" (p. 572).

I do read to know that I am not alone, I can see, going over these words I wrote down from reading, or at least such words do speak to my loneliness. There is much about God in these sayings. I can see how they relate to the four sentences I have culled from reading Tolkien: "Things are meant," "There are signs," "The heart speaks," "There is a way."[4] Like those four sentences, these sayings seem to carry a vision. I find myself looking for a vision in other kinds of reading too, for instance in reading the Summas of St. Thomas Aquinas, I find a peace in contemplating his vision of everything coming from God and then returning to God. It is like the vision carried by the words of the old Bedouin to Lawrence of Arabia, "The love is from God and of God and towards God."[5] It seems to say loneliness becomes love and loneliness itself is from God and of God and towards God. It is like the vision carried by the concluding words of Dante's *Divine Comedy*, "I felt myself moved by the love that moves the sun and the other stars."[6]

We read, then, to know we are not alone, to know our loneliness becomes love, to know the love is from God and of God and towards God. Let us see then what we learn of loneliness and love in reading, in passing over to others and coming back to ourselves. "That fruitful miracle of a communication in solitude," as Proust calls it, may be already a kind of learning to love.

Passing Over

When you pass over into the heart of another tradition, really into its heart, then indeed "heart speaks to heart." A. J. Arberry describes something like this in his experience of translating the Koran. "This task was undertaken, not lightly, and carried to its conclusion at a time of great personal distress," he says in his preface, "through which it comforted and sustained the writer in a manner for which he will always be grateful."[7] Translating can be a massive experience of passing over, but simply reading can be comforting and sustaining in a time of great personal distress, as translating was for Arberry, when there is a comforting and sustaining vision to be found in the writing. What makes such a vision? In the Koran the vision is conveyed already in the opening Sura: there is a God who is compassionate and merciful, and there is a way, a straight path. There is no mention of God in the four little sentences I culled from reading Tolkien, "Things are meant," "There are signs," "The heart speaks," "There is a way," but God is very implicit there, a God who is provident. And I do find that experience in reading Tolkien of being sustained and comforted in times of great personal distress.

There is a kind of writing that goes with reading, even when you are not translating, and that is writing in a diary or in a commonplace book. Writing in a journal is like keeping a ship's log, and it creates the sense of being on a voyage or a journey. Those four sentences I got from reading Tolkien actually spell out the sense of being on a journey: things happen and seem to be meaningful, to be "meant," as part of the voyage or journey, and there are signs along the way, pointing the way, and the heart speaks in response to the things and the signs, and there is a sure conviction there is a way, even when it seems there is no way. I remember, the second great enthusiasm of my childhood, after hearing and reading stories, was voyages and travels. I wanted to be a sea captain!

Voyages and travels, while being a kind of reading, have become a very real part of my life and a source of writing. There is a passing over that takes place in voyages and travels that is more massive and physical than that in reading, and those four sentences about things and signs and the heart and the way, arising from the sense of being on a journey, are *realized* in the chance meetings that occur on voyages and travels, for those chance meetings always seem to be more than chance and to have meaning of heart to heart, and to be signs of the way. Still, the journey of life is essentially a journey in time rather than from place to place. Voyages and travels are an image of the journey in time, and to "realize," as I read once in a dictionary of synonyms, is to "imagine vividly" something that is real, and that happens not only when I am voyaging and traveling but also when I am sitting quietly and reading. And when I am on my voyages and travels, if I don't "imagine vividly" the real things I encounter, then they will leave me unmoved.

There is a parable about voyages and travels in the *Odyssey*. When Odysseus visits the land of the dead, Tiresias the blind seer tells him "you must take an oar with you, and journey until you find men who do not know the sea . . . and when a wayfarer shall meet you and tell you that is a winnowing shovel on your shoulder, fix the oar in the ground, and make sacrifice"[8] first to the god of the sea and then come home and make sacrifice to all of the gods. What does the parable mean? After passing over in voyages and travels, I suppose, you must come back again to your home and go deep into your homeland, far from the sea. I think of a Sufi sheik I met on the Mount of Olives in Jerusalem who told me and two young Israeli women who were with me, "Go deep in your own religion!"[9]

Still, Odysseus was to go deep into his homeland only after his voyages and travels. Once, in conversation, Raimundo Pannikar told me he believed you began to really understand your own religion when you came to be acquainted with another. He himself was a living example of this: his father a Hindu, his mother a Catholic, and he himself a Catholic priest who was always thinking of Christianity and Hinduism in terms of each other. I gather that it is very important for me to pass over into other religions and to read their scriptures in order to come back with new insight to Christianity. I have to pass over before I come back and go deep, and I learn about this, coming back and going deep, like Odysseus, in the middle of my voyages and travels, in the middle of passing over.

My own odyssey of reading and traveling has been an experience of the mystical unity of the great religions. It is in coming back, though, and going deep in my own religion, in planting my oar deep in the heart of my homeland that I've come to perceive the uniqueness of Christianity. There is a common experience, common to all the great religions, it seems to me, and there are unique insights into that experience, unique to each religion. What is this common experience? There is a peace that is spoken of in all the religions, though it is difficult to describe except through the insight of one or another of the religions. Still, it is possible to experience the peace in the holy places of the religions, for instance in the Ayasofya in Istanbul, a church for a thousand years, a mosque for five hundred years, and now just an empty place where you can still feel the peace of thousands of years of prayer. It is possible to feel the peace reading, too, as well as traveling. I think of the opening words of each Sura of the Koran, "In the name of God, the Merciful, the Compassionate," and the opening words of the Diamond Sutra and the Heart Sutra, "Homage to the Perfection of Wisdom, the Lovely, the Holy."[10]

One of these two religions is older than Christianity, Buddhism, and one of them is younger, Islam. What am I learning from them? "Homage to the Perfection of Wisdom, the Lovely, the Holy." What is this wisdom? A story helps me, *The Snow Leopard*, Peter Matthiessen's log of his journey in the Himalayas to the Crystal Mountain. He tells of his hope of seeing a snow leopard. "If the snow leopard should manifest itself, then I am ready to see the snow leopard," he writes. "If not, then somehow (and I don't understand this instinct, even now) I am not ready to perceive it . . . and in the not-seeing I am content . . . that the snow leopard *is,* that it is here, that its frosty eyes watch us from the mountain—that is enough."[11] As it turns out, he never sees a snow leopard. What then is wisdom? Is it "seeing the snow leopard"? Or is it rather knowing the snow leopard *is* and knowing "that is enough"?

There is a wisdom also in that other invocation, "In the name of God, the Merciful, the Compassionate." It is the wisdom of "remembering God" (*dikhr Allah*). That invocation occurs not only at the beginning of each Sura of the Koran but also at the beginning of *A Thousand and One Nights.*[12] It is fitting, that seems to say, to remember God not only when praying and reciting the Koran but also when telling and listening to stories, in fact in all human activities. To remember God, to remember the mercy and compassion of God, is to be wise, to see whatever happens, whatever is said, whatever is told, to see all in the light of God, in the light of God's mercy and compassion. Here too a story helps me, *Seven Pillars of Wisdom,* and the encounter there of Lawrence of Arabia with the old Bedouin who told him, "The love is from God and of God and towards God." Wisdom is in the vision of that great circle coming from God and returning to God.

Wisdom for me is Ayasofya, the divine figure for whom the place is named, "Wisdom has built her house, she has set up her seven pillars," and I can say of her and to her, "Homage to the Perfection of Wisdom, the Lovely, the Holy," though in saying that I have perhaps gone beyond any valid interpretation of the Diamond Sutra or the Heart Sutra. Still, in a Buddhist-Christian dialogue on education once I told of the encompassing peace I felt there in the place called the Ayasofya and how I had come to call the figure of Wisdom by that name Ayasofya and the Buddhists in the group seemed to resonate strongly with my experience.[13] At that moment, all three religions seemed to meet, Buddhism, Christianity, and Islam. For Christianity and Islam had already met in that place, a church for a thousand years, a mosque for five hundred years, and now the name Hagia Sophia, "Holy Wisdom," Ayasofya in Turkish, seemed to resonate for Buddhists, who also recognize Holy Wisdom. Is this a mystical unity of the religions?

Or is it an illustration of the unique insight of each religion into a common experience?

It is the common experience, I believe, the encompassing peace, that is the mystical unity of the religions. The wisdom each religion finds in this peace is its own unique insight into the common experience. Thus I can also say "In the name of God, the Merciful, the Compassionate," but the God I am thinking of is the God of Jesus, the God he calls Abba. I believe that is one and the same God as the one Muslims call Allah, but a unique insight is conveyed in each of those names, a surpassing intimacy in the name Abba, a reverence touching your head to the ground in the name Allah. There is a unique relation with God in each religion or, to include Buddhism, let us say a unique relation with the Absolute. Passing over means entering into the unique relation by way of the common experience.

"Attention is the natural prayer of the soul,"[14] as Nicolas Malebranche says, and if I let prayer become more and more purely attention, I find myself passing over into something like Buddhism, and if, vice-versa, I let attention become more and more purely prayer, I find myself passing over into something like Islam. So when I do try to understand Buddhism, I do so by letting prayer become attention ("No snowflake ever falls in the wrong place.")[15] That enables me to read the Sutras. And when I try to understand Islam, I do so by letting attention become prayer ("remembering God"). That enables me to read the Suras.

I am accustomed to actually praying to Holy Wisdom, for instance in the words from the Liturgy of the Hours, "Wisdom of God, be with me, always at work in me."[16] Yet now to let prayer become more and more purely attention doesn't seem to violate an "I and thou" relationship with Holy Wisdom, changing the relation to "I and it," but simply to let Wisdom speak to me, and there are indeed sayings in these Buddhist wisdom books that speak to my heart. First, there is that invocation at the beginning of both the Diamond and the Heart Sutra, "Homage to the Perfection of Wisdom, the Lovely, the Holy," which is like my prayer to Holy

Wisdom. Then there are the words at the end of the Diamond Sutra, "As falling stars, a fault of vision, as a lamp, a mock show, dew drops, or a bubble, a dream, a lightning flash, or a cloud, so should one view what is conditioned."[17] I take these to be words like those of the Buddha that this little span of life is but a passing shadow, a fleeting thing, words that guide the heart away from attachment to passing things. And then there are the words at the end of the Heart Sutra, "Gone, gone, gone beyond, gone altogether beyond, O what an awakening, all hail!,"[18] words describing the discovery of the unconditioned, of the eternal.

Moving the other way, letting attention become more and more purely prayer, "remembering God," I think of that other invocation, "In the name of God, the Merciful, the Compassionate," and I think of the words of the Koran inscribed around the cupola of the Ayasofya where the light comes streaming through, "God is the Light of the heavens and the earth." The Light is the wisdom of Islam, the Light of God of the shining sky, and yet the Light is not the harsh light of the desert. It is the light of mercy and compassion. That speaks to my heart too: "the Merciful, the Compassionate" is "the Light of the heavens and the earth." The light in the Sura of the Koran called "Light" is the soft light of a lamp. "God is the Light of the heavens and the earth," Arberry translates, "the likeness of His Light is as a niche wherein is a lamp, the lamp in a glass, the glass as it were a glittering star."[19] That is the light of Holy Wisdom.

But "Who will exchange an old lamp for a new one?"[20] it is said in the story of Aladdin. Who will exchange an old insight for a new one? . . . a new insight for an old one? Passing over is limited by coming back. Without becoming a Buddhist, I will never fully understand Buddhism; and without becoming a Muslim, I will never fully understand Islam. Remaining a Christian as I am, my passing over into other religions is limited by my coming back again to Christianity. "Who will exchange an old lamp for a new one?" All the same, I do come back to Christianity with new insight from passing over. For others, though, who have gone over more fully, like Matthiesen in *The Snow Leopard,* like Lawrence (to the culture more than to the religion) in *Seven Pillars of Wisdom,* the opposite is true. "Who will exchange a new lamp for an old one?"

There is in passing over a "learned ignorance," as Nicolas Cusanus would say, and a "coincidence of opposites."[21] Passing over is like translating. In fact, there is translation in reading the sacred books of the great religions, from the Sanskrit in reading the Sutras, from the Arabic in reading the Suras, but the learned ignorance is not just in knowing something is lost in translation, or even in knowing just what is lost in translation ("poetry is what gets lost in translation," as Robert Frost says, hopefully not truth). It is in knowing I do not possess the "Perfection of Wisdom," although I do reverence Holy Wisdom and have a relationship with Holy Wisdom. It is in knowing I do not fully comprehend the mercy and the compassion of God, although I do reverence "the Merciful, the Compassionate" and have a relationship with God. Knowing I know would be certainty; knowing I do not know is openness to the mystery.

It is in letting prayer become more and more purely attention and in the opposite process of letting attention become more and more purely prayer that I find a "coincidence of opposites," I find "mysticism East and West" and something like a "transcendent unity of religions."[22] All I mean by such phrases, though, is to say "attention is the natural prayer of the soul." Each religion has its own practice of prayer or meditation that leads into the unique insight of the religion, but it is possible, I believe, to pass over into that insight in some degree simply in virtue of the common basis of attention, the natural prayer of the soul. Some years ago I attended meetings of Jews and Christians and Muslims in Jerusalem where we discussed prayer in the three religions, and found ourselves coming ever closer in understanding until the talk veered towards politics. More recently I had a similar experience at a meeting of Buddhists and Christians on education where in effect we discussed attention, the essence of study and prayer, as Simone

Weil says in *Waiting for God*,[23] and found ourselves coming to concord and mutual understanding.

It is attention that carries me to the heart of Buddhism, and it is prayer that carries me to the heart of Islam. What I find there, at the heart, is as Dag Hammarskjöld says, "We all have within us a center of stillness surrounded by silence."[24] Attention leaves me listening to the silence and very aware of the void at the center of stillness, the "no self" (*anatta*) of Buddhists, but prayer leads me to take the surrounding silence as the presence of God and to take the empty center of stillness as my own deeper "I" in relation to the divine "thou," as in the prayer of Jews and Christians and Muslims.

There is a common experience then, "We all have within us a center of stillness surrounded by silence," and there are equal and opposite interpretations of the experience, "no self" and "I and thou," equal and opposite but not actually contradictory. There is rather a "coincidence of opposites," a coinciding of opposite interpretations in the common experience of a center of stillness surrounded by silence. Perhaps we can say then there is a relation of complementarity between the two interpretations, between "no self" and "I and thou," somewhat as there is between particles and waves in the interpretation of physical phenomena. Consider, for instance, the meditation on the divine names in Islam. A Muslim friend, a professor at Istanbul University, was always fingering his beads as we talked, and on the last day when I was leaving he gave me his beads as a gift. I still have them, a precious gift, and I know the ninety-nine names of God that you recite and meditate on as you finger the beads, but as I learned from the story of al-Hallaj, put to death for saying "I am the Truth,"[25] you cannot ascribe one of these names to a human being. There is something incommunicable here, "I and thou" tips over into "no self" and "no self" tips over into "I and thou."

Al-Hallaj was standing in the nothingness of himself before God when he said "I am the Truth." His saying was an extreme statement of the creed, "There is no god but God," as if to say "There is no self but God," and thus "I and thou" tips over into "no self" and "no self" tips over into "I and thou." After beginning "We all have within us a center of stillness surrounded by silence," Hammarskjöld ends his little manifest for the United Nations Meditation Room, "There is an ancient saying that the sense of a vessel is not in its shell but in the void. So it is with this room. It is for those who come here to fill the void with what they find in their center of stillness."[26]

When I ask myself what I find in my own center of stillness, I am brought back again to myself. There are intimations of Christ and Christianity in the "coincidence of opposites" in al-Hallaj, and I am struck by Louis Massignon dedicating his lifework of forty years on al-Hallaj "to Jesus of Nazareth crucified king of the Jews" (*Iesu Nazareno Crucifixo Regi Judaeorum*),[27] and I find it easy to come back from this contemplation of the opposites in al-Hallaj, "no self" and "I and thou," and this hint that the divine names are communicable after all, to my own faith in Christ and Christianity. This mysterious "coincidence of opposites" inspires me to go deep in my own religion, to plant my oar deep in my homeland. Are the divine names communicable and can humans partake of the divine?

Coming Back

"Attention is the natural prayer of the soul" holds true for coming back as well as for passing over. What Malebranche had in mind was attention to the truth within us. "The attention of the spirit," he says, "is the natural prayer we make to the inner truth that it may disclose itself to us."[28] If I follow what he is saying, attention is to things as they appear to me when I am in my center of stillness surrounded by silence. They look very differently to me there than when I am off center, caught up in my fears and desires. So I go there to that peacefulness to make decisions, knowing my choices will be skewed if I am off center, but I go there also to read, to make possible "that fertile miracle of a communication effected in solitude," or reading brings me there, calming me and bringing me to inner repose even when I have been upset, and I am able to read there in the light of the "inner truth" (*la verite interieur*) that Malebranche speaks of and to see if that truth is disclosing itself in what I am reading.

I know Malebranche is speaking from a standpoint in which the soul is more closely united to God than it is to the body,[29] and thus the soul can learn directly from God. Still, what he is saying sounds very close to the Gospel of John, "No one can come to me unless the Father who sent me draws him. . . . It is written in the prophets, 'And they shall all be taught by God.' Every one who has heard and learned from the Father comes to me."[30] The controversial thing is Malebranche seeming to deny what follows, "Not that anyone has seen the Father except him who is from God." But it seems to me he is saying, like Saint Augustine, we see in God's light, and so we pray the inner truth to disclose itself, because it has not disclosed itself fully to us, and we pray again and again, because it reveals itself only step by step, insight by insight.

"We see only things, only objects, not light," the modern physicist says, thus "catching the light,"[31] for if light passes through space but there are no objects we see only darkness, and the same I believe is true of the inner light, we see things *in* the inner light, we do not see the inner light itself. Saint Augustine has become the archetypal Christian reader with the story he tells in his *Confessions* of his moment of conversion in the garden, hearing the words "Take and read." His method of reading after this became a method of reading in the inner light, in the light of the eternal truth present within us, his theory of illumination. If I understand him rightly, he is not saying we see the inner light but rather we see things *in* the inner light. Thus the point of reading is to bring things before our minds and let the inner light shine on them. The same thing happens in conversation. "If both of us see what you say is true and that what I say is true, then where, I ask, do we see this?" he says in his *Confessions.* "I do not see it in you, nor you in me, but both of us see it in the immutable truth which is higher than our minds."[32]

"An endless conversation,"[33] that was Diogenes' description of Plato's philosophy. A conversation that becomes a conversation with self, that is Augustine in his *Soliloquies,* and a conversation with self that becomes a conversation with God, that is Augustine in his *Confessions.* Reading, therefore, and especially reading aloud, as he apparently did, takes on these dimensions of a conversation with self, for Augustine, and a conversation with God. If I follow him in my own way, I let my heart speak to me as I am reading (silently like Ambrose), and as I let my heart speak I am letting God speak. "May I know me, may I know thee,"[34] he prayed already in his *Soliloquies,* and I too can hope to know me, to know thee in "that fertile miracle of a communication effected in solitude."

I have become convinced we love with a love we do not know, and when we read the Gospel we come to know the love we do not know. Let me begin at the end, with a conversation that takes place at the end of the Gospel of John. "Simon, son of John, do you love me more than these?" Jesus asks, and Simon Peter replies "Yes, Lord, you know that I love you."[35] But if we look at the Greek, we find here two different words for love. Jesus is asking *agapas me?* "Do you love me?" but with the great love, with *agape,* the unconditional love of God. And Simon Peter is answering *philo se,* "I am your friend," as if to say my love is that of *philia* or friendship. Then Jesus repeats the question, and Simon Peter repeats the answer, and then, the third time around, Jesus changes to the verb Simon Peter is using and asks *phileis me?* "Are you my friend?" And Simon Peter is very upset that his friendship is called into question, and he answers "Lord, you know everything, you know I am your friend" (*philo se*). Then Jesus goes on to speak of Simon Peter's future, how he will lay down his life and thus will indeed love with the great love (*agape*) that lays down life, and he ends saying "Follow me!"

There is another word for love in the *Dialogues* of Plato, and that is *eros* or "longing," the heart's longing.[36] If I bring that word from "an endless conversation" into the conversation here, then there are three names of love, Eros and Philia and Agape, and I can busy myself contrasting them or I can see them as stages on love's way, stages in coming to know love. All our loves are one love, I have come to believe, the love of God, and when we are heart and soul in love it becomes transparently the love of God. So Agape is the true name of love, and this I think I learn from reading the Gospel.

Coming back means coming back to my own life and times and it is there, in the context of my own life and times, that I read the Gospel, and so when I read of Agape I think of the words of the old Bedouin to Lawrence, "The love is from God and of God and towards God," I think of a great circle of love coming from God and returning to God, and I ponder in this light the two questions that are asked of Jesus in the Gospel of John, "Where do you come from?" and "Where are you going?" And when I read the opening words, "In the beginning was the Word," I think also of the closing words of *The Death of Virgil* by Hermann Broch, "it was the word beyond speech."[37] I think again of the great circle of love and now I see how the other metaphors used in the Gospel of John are included. It is a great circle of life and of light and of love, and though the Word is a "word beyond speech" it does seem to speak to my heart whenever my life opens up before me all the way to death. I seem to understand what Simon Peter means when he says "you have the words of eternal life."[38]

When I read the other gospels then, Matthew, Mark, and Luke, I take the words of Jesus there too as "words of eternal life." Is my reading then completely uncritical? What of the sayings ascribed to Jesus in the Gospel of Thomas? Nowadays those sayings, mostly paradoxes, are often taken as criteria of the sayings of Jesus, so that those in the canonical gospels are judged authentic or unauthentic according to their relation to these paradoxes. For me the only adequate criterion is the one mentioned in the Gospel of John, "My teaching is not mine, but his who sent me; if any man's will is to do his will, he shall know whether the teaching is from God or whether I am speaking on my own authority."[39] The sayings of Jesus then have to be judged in the light of a willingness to do God's will.

"His will is our peace" (*la sua voluntate e nostra pace*),[40] Dante's maxim, is a kind of criterion of choice, when I am trying to discern and decide my way in life. When I am in my center of stillness surrounded by silence, I am able to see my way where I cannot when I am off center, caught up in desires and fears. The willingness to do God's will seems to be the necessary and sufficient condition of being in that peace, and "His will is our peace" thus seems a criterion for judging sayings about the way just as it is for finding the way or finding the next step on the way. There seems to be an assumption or implication here that the will of God for us and our own deepest heart's longing are one and the same, thus the peace of being willing to do God's will, and there is in *The Divine Comedy* a vision of love in which the heart's longing becomes by way of human love, like that of Dante and Beatrice, "the love that moves the sun and the other stars" (*l'amor che move il sole e l'altre stelle*).

Well, I am reading the Gospel in the light of everything else I have read, mentioning sentences like these, "it was the word beyond speech" and "his will is our peace" and "The love is from God and of God and towards God" and phrases like "the love that moves the sun and the other stars." I realize too, as I do this, that I am passing over in reading the Gospel and coming back to everything else I have read, seeing everything I have read in the light of the Gospel.

"We are to do nothing but wait," Heidegger says of thinking, and that could be said also of reading, especially of reading the Gospel. "Then what are we to wait for? And where are we to wait? I hardly know any more who and where I am" says the Scientist in "A Conversation on a Country Path." "None of us knows that, as soon as we stop fooling ourselves," the Teacher replies. "And yet we still have our path?"[41] the Scholar adds. So it is with reading the Gospel, it seems to me, I come to the Gospel as if "I hardly know any more who and where I am" and I let the Gospel tell me who and where I am. I am waiting, as I am reading, to learn who and where I am, and yet I still have my path and that is to walk with

Matthew, Mark, Luke, and John, even to walk with Thomas, and as I walk with them I have a sense of being led. "Ever more openly I am coming to trust in the inconspicuous guide who takes us by the hand—or better said, by the word—in this conversation," the Scientist says, and so it is in reading, especially in reading the Gospel. It is "the night having set in, which without forcing compels concentration"[42] that is the guide in "A Conversation on a Country Path." I take it "the inconspicuous guide" in reading the Gospel is something more, the very Spirit that was in Jesus and passes into his disciples.

Actually the guide in "A Conversation on a Country Path" seems to be at times the night and at times the course of the conversation. "The occasion which led me to let myself into waiting in the way mentioned was more the course of the conversation,"[43] the Scientist says, and the Scholar comments on how fitting this is, and the Teacher adds "Above all when the occasion is as inconspicuous as the silent course of a conversation that moves us."[44] Then later the Scientist says "It seems to me that this unbelievable night entices you both to exult."[45] When the question arises, who introduced the term "letting be" (Gelassenheit) into the conversation, "Then who did it? None of us?" the Scholar asks, "Presumably," the Teacher replies, "for in the region in which we stay everything is in the best order only if it has been no one's doing . . . because it is the region of the word, which is answerable to itself alone."[46]

Likewise in reading the gospel, "the inconspicuous guide" is the Word, like "the course of the conversation" in "the region of the word," and yet also the Spirit, like "the night," "this unbelievable night." I find the Word in the prologues of John to his gospel and to his first letter, and I find the Spirit in the prologues of Luke, reading that of his gospel side by side with that of Acts.

"Be patient toward all that is unsolved in your heart,"[47] Rilke says, and I find I have to do that in letting the Word guide me, if "it was the word beyond speech" and not simply some spoken or written word like Gelassenheit belonging to "the region of the word." I can see that wisdom for me is not simply to let be and be open to the mystery, as in "A Conversation on a Country Path," but to know "we can know more than we can tell"[48] and to listen for that "more" in what is told in the Gospels. Christianity "presents salvation to human beings in a person rather than a doctrine,"[49] as Pierre Rousselot says, and thus the Word is a person rather than a doctrine. There are the words of Jesus as well as his person, to be sure, and these words are in the form of sayings and stories, and there is a doctrine in what is said and told, but if I come to these words with "all that is unsolved in my heart" I find there "the word beyond speech."

Taking the Word as a person rather than a doctrine, I have to enter into the relation of Jesus with God in order to understand him, I have to enter into "unconditional relation" as Buber calls it in *I and Thou.* "For it is the *I* of unconditional relation in which the man calls his *Thou* Father in such a way that he himself is simply Son, and nothing else but Son," Buber says of Jesus, but he goes on to say "every one can say *Thou* and is then *I,* every one can say Father and is then Son: reality abides."[50] So I too can say *Thou* and am then *I,* can say Father and am then Son. As Buber understands this, from the standpoint of Judaism, I am entering into a relation *like* that of Jesus with God. As I understand it, from the standpoint of Christianity, I am entering into the very relation of Jesus with God and so he is *present* in me, "I live, yet not I, but Christ lives in me."[51]

Entering into this "I and thou" with God, I am entering into a stance of prayer and bringing "all that is unsolved in my heart" to God in prayer. Here again "attention is the natural prayer of the soul" and I pay attention to all the words of the gospel, hoping they will speak somehow to "all that is unsolved in my heart." I see the Spirit that was in Jesus at work in this. "Likewise the Spirit helps us in our weakness," Paul writes to the Romans, "for we do not know how to pray as we ought, but the Spirit himself intercedes for us with sighs too deep for words."[52] What is unsolved in my heart? Well, I suppose it has to do especially with "the road not taken" in my life. I have taken a road in life, but there is a road or roads I have not taken and I am haunted by what I have seemingly lost. I look to the Gospel then, the "good tidings," to find grace is infinite, to find the roads of life rejoining somehow in an abundant life.

To be patient toward all that is unsolved in my heart is indeed to let be and be open to the mystery, as I learn from "A Conversation on a Country Path," but I seem to learn something more from the Gospel. It is as Kierkegaard says in *Fear and Trembling,* "in resignation I make renunciation of everything . . . by faith I make renunciation of nothing . . . by faith I acquire everything."[53] Resignation or "infinite resignation," as he calls it, is the element of *willingness* in faith, but there is also another element in faith, the element of *hope.* There are times in my life when I have to practice resignation, simply letting be and being open to the mystery, as for instance when a friend withdraws from my life and from our friendship.

Being open to the mystery that "shows itself and at the same time withdraws" in a person or in the things of my life is where willingness overlaps with hope. What then is my hope? "I am with you," the divine presence. Or that is what feels like an answer to me when I am having to let go of a human presence in my life. "I am with you": I see this in the "I am" sayings of Jesus, not only in the Gospel of John where they are particularly prominent but in Matthew and Mark and Luke as well, for instance in the story of walking on water where Jesus says "Don't be afraid, I am."[54] The "I am" sayings are somewhat hidden in the translations "It is I" and "I am he." I follow here the interpretation of my friend David Daube, who reads the Gospel in the light of the Talmud and takes the "I am" sayings as expressing the Shekinah, the divine presence. Reading the sayings from a Jewish standpoint, David takes them as transcendent, not personal. Jesus is not saying "*I* am," pointing to himself, but *I am,* pointing to the divine presence.[55] Reading them from a Christian standpoint, I take them as both transcendent and personal.

I know that "deconstruction" as practiced in our times by Jacques Derrida and Paul DeMan is a critique of "the metaphysics of presence,"[56] as it is called, where the presence of the speaker gives the spoken word a primacy over the written word. The presence that I am finding in the written word, especially in the "I am" sayings, can readily be deconstructed, shown to fail when it comes to conveying the presence of the speaker in the spoken word. There is even a famous deconstruction of "I am" by Arthur Rimbaud well before Derrida and DeMan, where Rimbaud writes perversely *Je est un autre* instead of *Je suis,* "I is another" instead of "I am."[57]

I find myself looking rather to "real presences" in life, as George Steiner calls them, when I am reading, in order to understand what I am reading. "We read to know that we are not alone," I agree, and above all when we are reading the Gospel, for then we read to know "God is with us" as the name Emmanuel implies. "All this took place to fulfill what the Lord had spoken by the prophet: Behold a virgin shall conceive and bear a son, and his name shall be called Emmanuel, which means, God with us."[58]

I know, Proust says reading is not a conversation with the minds of the past, as Ruskin maintained, there is not the give and take, the to-and-fro of conversation in reading, and so there is an element of absence, but it is nevertheless "that fertile miracle of a communication in solitude," and so there is an element of presence after all, insofar as communication can be effected even in solitude. Machiavelli used to dress in his finest clothes and go every night into his study to read and commune with the minds of the past, even to converse with them. "I am not ashamed to speak with them," he writes, "and to ask them the reason for their actions; and they in their kindness answer me; four hours may pass and I do not feel boredom, I forget every trouble, I do not dread poverty, I am not frightened by death; I give myself over entirely to them."[59] This is what I call "passing over." And so it is with Christ, I believe, in reading the Gospel, if I do not converse with him as the disciples did, at least I commune with him. But for someone like me who believes he is alive and lives in us, reading becomes conversing as well as communing, and that is what is meant by *lectio divina,* divine reading.

Divine Reading

*The love of learning
and the desire for God*
—Jean Leclercq

"My name and yours, and the true name of the sun, or a spring of water, or an unborn child, all are syllables of the great word that is very slowly spoken by the shining of the stars,"[1] Ursula LeGuin writes in one of her stories. There is something universal about the prologue to the Gospel of John, something that speaks not only to Christians but to others as well, "In the beginning was the Word. . . ." The parting of the ways comes, as Augustine pointed out,[2] in the words that follow, "And the Word was made flesh. . . ."

It is true, Goethe has Faust write "In the beginning was the Act"[3] instead of "In the beginning was the Word," and that goes with setting the active life over the contemplative life. If I read out of the peacefulness of the contemplative life, though, I am ready to agree, "In the beginning was the Word." I read, like the monks, out of "the love of learning and the desire for God,"[4] and that, I believe, is the method of "divine reading," *lectio divina,* reading out of our "center of stillness surrounded by silence." It has become a literary device, since Goethe, to write variations on the theme of the Word and the beginning. "A philosophy of communications conceives the message as order, meaning or unit," Michel Serres says in his *Genesis,* "but it also conceives the background noise from which it emerges,"[5] and thus prior to the word or message there is the noise. If we read in our "center of stillness surrounded by silence," though, the word seems to come out of silence and to return into silence.

Contemplative life is the missing dimension of life in our times. We have the active life and the life of enjoyment but we lack the contemplative life. All the same, "we all have within us a center of stillness surrounded by silence," and one way to the center is Serres' method of listening to the background noise, for instance listening to the "sea noise"[6] as he calls it, the pounding of the surf on the seashore. I see his method of reading Genesis as a method also of reading the Gospel, especially that of John, though one does not come to the beginning until the end, when one comes at last to silence, and then in the silence one is able to hear the Word. Serres in his *Genesis* goes through a series of free associations much as one might do in one's mind as one reads the opening words of the Bible, "In the beginning. . . ." One comes at last, though, to silence, and then the Word can speak. Or else the silence itself can speak.

What follows is my own reading, not listening to background noise so much as to the surrounding silence in our center of stillness, not seeking information, the other main category in information theory besides noise, so much as insight. "I begin to fathom the sound and the fury, of the world and of history: the *noise,*"[7] Serres writes. I begin to fathom the silence, I want to say, the silence out of which the Word comes and into which the Word returns.

The Word and the Music

"Wherever we are, what we hear is mostly noise,"[8] the composer John Cage says in *Silence.* "When we ignore it, it disturbs us.

When we listen to it, we find it fascinating." Listening to the background noise and finding it fascinating, as Serres does in his *Genesis,* listening to it as the composer John Cage does and finding it musical, Serres says "In the beginning is the song."[9] But what if we listen to the silence? Then we are ready to hear of a Word that is not other than music, of a music that is not other than the Word. Then I do believe we are ready to hear the prologue of John, "In the beginning was the Word. . . ." And when we come to the parting of the ways, "And the Word was made flesh . . . ," we are ready to hear that other prologue of John,

> What was from the beginning,
> what we have heard,
> what we have seen with our eyes,
> what we have looked upon,
> and our hands have handled,
> of the Word of life. . . .[10]

I think of another, very different, reading of the Gospel, that of Albert Schweitzer in *The Quest of the Historical Jesus:*

> There is silence all around. The Baptist appears, and cries: 'Repent, for the kingdom of heaven is at hand.' Soon after that comes Jesus, and in the knowledge that he is the coming Son of Man lays hold of the wheel of the world to set it moving on that last revolution which is to bring all ordinary history to a close. It refuses to turn, and he throws himself upon it. Then it does turn; and crushes him. Instead of bringing in the eschatological conditions, he has destroyed them. The wheel rolls onward, and the mangled body of the one immeasurably great man, who was strong enough to think of himself as the spiritual ruler of mankind and to bend history to his purposes, is hanging upon it still. That is his victory and his reign.[11]

Consider the differences. The prologue of John is about beginning, but this is about ending. The prologue is about the Word of life, but this is about the mangled body of death.

As I meditate on these contrasts, I am led back to read the prologue to the Gospel and to hear its music:

> In the beginning was the Word,
> and the Word was with God,
> and the Word was God.
> This was in the beginning with God;
> all came to be through this,
> and without this nothing came
> that ever came to be.
> In this was life,
> and the life was the light of humankind,
> and the light shines in the darkness,
> and the darkness has not overshadowed it.[12]

I was reading the prologue aloud in Greek as I translated and was trying to keep the rhythm in English. The first lines are as usual in the King James and the Revised Standard Version, but in the middle lines I have written "this" instead of "he," translating *outos* (and *autos* referring back to *outos*), thinking of the Word rather than of the Word incarnate. But in the last lines I am thinking of the Word incarnate and of what Schweitzer said above, and when I came to *katelaben* I used Peter Levi's "overshadowed."[13] For what I see in these last lines is not the mangled body hanging still on the wheel of the world but a presence like that in the last line of Matthew's Gospel, "I am with you always, even to the end of time."[14] And as I read aloud, I can see "In the beginning is the song," the prologue itself is a song, and I can set it to music. I will set it to music.

When you set words to music, you learn new things about the words themselves, and if a word or a phrase is weak and you are not bound to the wording, if you are the poet or if you are the translator, the music can lead you to a better wording just by the necessities of singing. But where does the music come from? I think of Mozart's *Ave Verum*, where he is setting words not unlike these but about the Eucharistic body of Christ, the presence in the form of bread and wine.[15] I can sing these words to his melody.

Looking for musical settings of the prologue of John, I find it is rarely set to music, but I have found a setting by Josquin Desprez, a Latin motet in four voices, *In Principio Erat Verbum*.[16] The words I have translated correspond to the first part of the motet. Then follows the second part, "There was a man sent from God, whose name was John . . . ," and then the third part, "And the Word was made flesh. . . ." One difference appears in the Latin translation, *quod factum est in ipso vita erat,* "whatever came to be in him was life," my seventh and eighth lines run together, with the thought that everything created existed as life in the Word. The Latin can be read the other way, separating the two lines, but Josquin clearly reads it this way, running the two together in a single musical phrase. There are three themes here: word, genesis, and light, and the three overlap, word and genesis in "This was in the beginning with God" (the Latin too uses *hoc,* "this," instead of *hic,* "he"), and genesis and light in the life containing all things created, "and the life was the light."

"He is the master of the notes," Luther said of Josquin; "others are mastered by them,"[17] and a music critic of our day says "For a superb example of Josquin's later four-part style . . . we need look no further than *In Principio Erat Verbum*. . . . The texture is as transparent as ever, with its preponderance of duets, and characteristically it makes continuous reference to the underlying recitation tone, but with a variety of texture and an impetus informing the austerity that makes it possible to cover fourteen verses of St. John's Gospel with no hint of monotony."[18] I am intimidated, but I know I will learn something if I try to set my own translation to music.

I think of a melody that came to me long ago when I was studying in Rome, a melody I imagined played by the cellos, and so here I will give it to the baritone voice. The melody came to me, though, long before I tried to translate the words. So it is true, "In the beginning is the song." I think also of a higher counter melody that went with it. These two melodies fit the words very well and fall readily into song form, ABC where C = A. I think of the

In the Beginning Was the Word

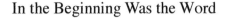

melodies, therefore, in the bass and I think of a repeating figure in the treble of three tones but in four/four time and changing thus in beat and in harmony with the melodies. So the texture is somewhat minimalist, like that of piano pieces by John Adams, his *Phrygian Gates* and *China Gates*,[19] but here there are no "gates," changes of mode, and of course the texture is changed by the presence of the voice. The sound, beginning pianissimo in the treble, then mezzoforte with the voice, is serene and it does seem to carry the mystery of the beginning.

What, then, do I learn from setting the words to music? Casting the words into song form, ABC where C = A, I have three themes,

A = the Word, B = the Word of life, and C = the light in the dark-ness, and, because this last theme is the same as the first in music, I have taken the words "And the light shines in the darkness and the darkness has not overshadowed it" as the same theme as the words "In the beginning was the Word, and the Word was with God, and the Word was God." I imagine the connection is with the words "Let there be light" in Genesis, the first words uttered by God in the Bible. God creates by letting be, and primarily by letting there be light, and the Word is "Let there be" and "Let there be light" and the life in the Word is the light that shines in the darkness.

There is a fragment of the early Greek philosopher Heraclitus that is about the Logos, and that has been much discussed as a forerunner of the Logos of John's prologue. One main question has been whether to translate Logos here, too, as Word. If we leave the crucial word Logos untranslated, we can translate the saying as follows:

> Listening not to me but to the Logos,
> you are (it is) wise to confess One is All.[20]

Heidegger has made much of this saying and paraphrases this way:

> Do not listen to me, the mortal speaker, but be in hearkening to the Laying that gathers; first belong to this and then you hear properly; such hearing *is* when a letting-lie-together-before occurs by which the gathering letting-lie, the Laying that gathers, lies before us as gathered; when a letting-lie of the letting-lie-before occurs, the fateful comes to pass; then the truly fateful, i.e., destiny alone, is the unique One unifying All.[21]

Logos is a noun connected with the Greek verb *legein,* which means to gather or to speak. What Heidegger is doing here is going with the first meaning, to gather, rather than the second, to speak. The two meanings may be connected, nevertheless, as when I *gather* my wits before I *speak.* Logos, then, is a gathering and a speaking. What Heraclitus is talking about is listening, thus listening to something that can be heard, to a word or message, or to background noise like the sea noise. Whatever it is, what comes of listening is confessing or acknowledging (*omologein*) One is All, or All is One (*En Panta*). The *logein* in *omologein* incidentally gives us the intended etymology of *logos,* a gathering and a speaking that can be listened to and responded to in acknowledgment. The response in words is "One is All" or "All is One."

What Michel Serres finds, listening to the background noise, is not the One but the Many, "the multiple as such,"[22] he says. Listening myself to the background noise, to the sea noise, I listen for what I hear when I listen to the silence surrounding my center of stillness. I hearken to an encompassing Presence. So for me it does seem wise to acknowledge "One is All" or "All is One." It is true, nevertheless, if I listen for the "gathering" as well as the "speaking" in the Word or the Presence, then I get a sense of the Many, "the multiple as such," brought together in the One. The Word then is the Alpha and the Omega, the Word in the beginning and the Word at the end, the One in the Many and the Many in the One.

I think of the ideas of Teilhard de Chardin, set out in *The Divine Milieu* and *The Phenomenon of Man,* "everything that rises must converge,"[23] everything that rises in the Alpha must converge in the Omega. I think his ideas are due for reconsideration, his idea especially of the Omega as the presence of Christ in the world leading the world to its consummation. The word *parousia* in the New Testament is usually translated "coming" but its prime meaning is "presence" as in "I am with you always, even to the end of time." All this I see and feel in the words and music, "And the light shines in the darkness, and the darkness has not over-shadowed it."

There is a practice of the Presence, very like the practice of the present, "To cast aside regret and fear," as Tolkien says, "To do the deed at hand."[24] I am not easily able to let go of regret and fear (I am trying at this very moment to let go). It is only a sense of the Presence that enables me to do so, a sense of "I am with you," and that seems to depend on believing in the Presence, believing "I am with you." If I can believe in the words "I am with you," I can feel the Presence. It is those words that illumine the silence surrounding me in my center of stillness, and it is the inner light of faith that illumines the words that illumine the silence. The words are "the words of eternal life" for me, and the Presence I can feel in the surrounding silence is "the Word of life," and in the strength of the words, in the strength of the Presence, I am able to "cast aside regret and fear," I am able to "do the deed at hand." The crucial thing is the inner light of faith. The Quakers call it the Inner Light, or the Light Within, or the Christ Within. It is my experience of "the light shines in the darkness, and the darkness has not overshadowed it."

Now there is a relation here between words and music. Once there was a unity of words and music in what was called *musike* in Greek and *musica* in Latin, where the rhythm of the words was actually musical. Then there was a separation of the two, a differentiation of words and music, each evolving on its own path, and that permitted the development of prose and of music as we know it. Now it seems to me the time is ripe for a reunion of words and music, not a revival of the old *musike* or *musica* so much as an integration of words and music as we have come to know them in their differentiation. The Word was proclaimed in "the prose of the Gospel"[25] as Thrasybulos Georgiades calls it, contrasting it with the music of the the *Iliad* and the *Odyssey*. But now, it seems, it is time to listen for the music of the Gospel, the music of the Word.

It may be that the separation of words and music goes with a separation of this world from the otherworld, as Georgiades says, and thus a reunion of words and music would go with a vision of one world, as in Paul Claudel's *Tidings Brought to Mary,*

> "Did you mean this world? Or is there another?"
> "There are two of them and I tell you there is
> only one of them and it is enough."[26]

There is only one world, Claudel is saying, but this one world contains in itself both this world and the otherworld. Thinking myself also of "the many worlds interpretation"[27] of modern quantum physics, I want also to say there is only one world with respect to the many possible worlds of physical reality. What I have in mind is a contemplative reading of the Gospel, somewhat like that envisioned by Proust in his essay *On Reading.* "Often, in St. Luke's Gospel, meeting with the colons that interrupt it before each of the almost canticle-like passages with which it is strewn," Proust says, "I have heard the silence of the worshipper who had just stopped from reading it aloud in order to intone the verses following, like a psalm that reminded him of the more ancient psalms of the Bible."[28]

One world, if it is twofold or manifold, requires a harmony of its many elements. John Adams, the American composer, speaks of a vision or dream of Meister Eckhart with a child on his shoulder telling him the secret of grace, and the secret, Adams believes, is harmony.[29] "Nothing exists without music," Isidore of Seville said; "for the universe itself is said to have been framed by a kind of harmony of sounds, and heaven itself revolves under the tones of that harmony."[30] So even if the Gospel is in prose, it seems to call for music. Instead of a "wave function of the universe" where there are as many worlds as there are possible solutions, there is the one Word. It is as if God spoke one Word and then kept silence, as Saint John of the Cross said,[31] for in that one Word God was able to say everything. I come to music, therefore, listening for the Word but also listening to the silence.

It is as if music without words were prayer without words, and music with words were prayer with words, and listening to silence were listening to music without words. In his last works Beethoven seems to say something about words and music. Symphonies are usually without words, but his last has words at the end, those of an Ode to Joy. And string quartets are usually without words, but his last has words at the beginning of its last movement, set to a simple melody, "Must it be? It must be! It must be!"[32] The words of the Gospel are without music, but they seem to call for music, especially if we think of them as "words of eternal life" giving expression to the one "Word of life." There is a silence, as Proust says, between the words. In listening to the silence, he is listening to the past, to "the ancient soul," to "a silence many centuries old,"[33] but the believer, listening to the silence, is listening to the eternal, taking time and the flow of words as "a changing image of eternity."[34]

If God spoke one Word, God also spoke many words contained in the one Word, for instance the ten commandments are called in Hebrew "the ten words," and if God keeps silence, it is only apart from the Word that continues to speak and to be heard. So I listen then for the Word and for the silence from which the Word comes and into which the Word returns. That silence is in our experience of having, every one of us, "a center of stillness surrounded by silence," and if I take that surrounding silence as an encompassing presence, then the silence seems to speak and to say "I am with you." So that for me is the Word that comes out of the silence and returns into the silence. The Word conveys the Presence.

It is by means of the Presence, Martin Buber says, that God guides us on our way. "The guiding counsel of God seems to me to be simply the divine Presence," he says, "communicating itself direct to the pure in heart."[35] Thus when I ask God to show me the way, instead of specific instructions, I experience simply the silent Presence of God, as if God were saying "I am with you." All the same there is direction in this and in the Scriptures and particularly in the Gospels. "Love is a direction,"[36] as Simone Weil says, a direction that becomes more specific when I take into account "the particulars of my life,"[37] as Shakespeare calls them. It is as though there were "songlines" in the Gospel—not indeed actual lines on the map accompanied by folksongs describing the journey, as among the Australian aborigines. The songlines of the Gospel are the ways time's arrow from past to future can become love's direction "from God and of God and towards God." The lines of time's arrow and love's direction are accompanied by sayings and stories of the Gospel as the aboriginal songlines are accompanied by journey songs.

Music is a metaphor then, if I speak of the songlines of the Gospel. If I take the songlines as my guide, nevertheless, I am letting time's arrow become love's direction in my life, letting myself be guided by the sayings and stories of the Gospel. I remember something my friend Martin Versfeld said in his last years, that he wanted to focus on sayings and stories, looking to them rather than to systematic thought for wisdom. It is not that these sayings and stories are a complete expression of the Word. Instead there are many situations in which the Word must speak to us anew if we are to find our way. I think of a saying of Tolkien's, "For even

the very wise cannot see all ends."[38] So too the wisdom of the sayings and the stories cannot see all ends, though that of "the word
beyond speech" can.

I don't know how things are going to come out in my life. "I
wonder what sort of a tale we've fallen into?" Sam muses aloud in
Tolkien's trilogy. "I wonder," Frodo says. "But I don't know. And
that's the way of a real tale. Take any one that you're fond of. You
may know, or guess, what kind of a tale it is, happy-ending or sad-
ending, but the people in it don't know. And you don't want them
to."[39] Being in the story of my life, I don't know how it will come
out. If I follow the songlines of the Gospel, I know at least that
I am on a road that does not dead-end. "The Road goes ever on,"
as in the theme song of Tolkien's song cycle, "until it joins some
larger way, where many paths and errands meet, and whither then?
I cannot say."[40]

The Restless Reader

Not knowing how things will come out, and yet knowing the
true way does not dead-end, I look for road signs, for signs of the
Road that goes ever on. In *The Songlines* Bruce Chatwin asks
searching questions: Why are we the most restless, dissatisfied of
animals? Why do wandering people conceive the world as perfect
whereas sedentary ones always try to change it? Why have the great
teachers—Christ or the Buddha—recommended the Road as the
way to salvation? Do we agree with Pascal that all our troubles
stem from our inability to sit quietly in a room?[41] As I reflect on
the answers I have learned to these questions, how our heart is
restless until it rests in God, how a traveler's vision differs from
that of a dweller, how our life is a journey in time, how we all
have within us a center of stillness surrounded by silence, I begin
to see how the signs spoken of in the Gospel of John, especially in
the first twelve chapters, sometimes called The Book of Signs, are
signs of God at work in the world, still at work and not yet at rest
on the sabbath. It is as if we were still in the sixth day of creation,

when God is at work creating human beings, and have not yet come to the eternal sabbath.

It takes a lifetime to create a human being, and we cooperate in our own creation, seeing, saying, doing what God is doing. "My Father is working still, and I am working," Jesus says in the Gospel of John, explaining why he heals on the sabbath, for "the Son can do nothing of his own accord, but only what he sees the Father doing."[42] He reveals God by doing humanly what God is doing, and we too are able to do what God is doing, for "one who believes in me will also do the works that I do."[43] God creates by letting be, by knowing and loving us into being, illumining our minds and kindling our hearts, and we are able to cooperate in creation by letting be ourselves, by coming ourselves to know and to love.

Somehow the key to the questions Chatwin asks about restlessness and wandering and the way and sitting quietly in a room is in a willingness to walk alone, not a will to walk alone that would exclude companions, but a willingness that welcomes company and yet can be without it, that walks and yet can sit, that rests in restlessness. It is a willingness to walk with God who is at work in the world, not yet resting. I see hints of this in the words of Jesus before healing the blind man, "We must work the works of him who sent me, while it is day; night comes, when no one can work," and before raising Lazarus from the dead, "Are there not twelve hours in the day? If any one walks in the day, he does not stumble, because he sees the light of this world. But if any one walks in the night, he stumbles, because the light is not in him."[44] God is at work, but in the light ("Let there be light") not in the darkness, and still "the light shines in the darkness, and the darkness has not overshadowed it."

What does it mean to say "night comes"? Does it mean death is coming? Some of the later years in Dag Hammarskjöld's diary *Markings* begin with the words "Night is drawing nigh."[45] If I see my life as a journey with God in time, the Road goes ever on and on, does not dead-end, and yet death comes to me on the Road. It is as if two figures were walking side by side, but in the distance they meld into one figure. In life I am side by side with God; in death I am in God who is still walking on and on.

To rest in restlessness therefore is to do what God is doing, bringing human beings into being. It is willingly to be in becoming, letting be as God does in creating. I think this is what Pierre de Caussade means by *L'abandon* in his classic *Abandonment to Divine Providence*.[46] The abandon he speaks of is a letting be that lets be the divine letting be. By letting my own restlessness be I come to rest in it and I come into accord with what is happening in my life. I can get stuck on one thing, for instance someone or something I have lost, and ignore everything else that enters and passes in my life. Abandon here means letting go of the obsession with one in order to live all, to find divine providence in all of them. My restlessness is a movement that carries me from one thing to another and it gets interrupted if I get stuck on one thing. If I rest in the restless movement, I go with the stream of my consciousness and I find there a process that can well be called *genesis*, an emergence of meaning out of what seems otherwise a background of chaos.

Coming and going, that is essentially what Jesus is doing in the Gospel of John, coming from God and going to God. The signs of the coming are the bread and the wine, the water of life, the healing of the sick child, of the paralytic, of the blind man. The signs of the going are the cleansing of the temple, his prophesied death and resurrection, and the death and resurrection of Lazarus. The essential, though, is the coming and the going itself. We too come and go: I come into time and I go into eternity. "Walk on!"[47] Buddha's last word to his disciples seems to apply, "Walk on!"

"And if you should lose each other," the Lady in the Forest says to Mossy and Tangle in *The Golden Key*, "do not be afraid, but go on and on."[48] There is a sadness in losing each other, a sadness that is not easily thrown off or left behind. Here is where a willingness to walk alone becomes essential. "The hour is coming, indeed it has come, when you will be scattered, every man to his home, and you will leave me alone," Jesus says at the Last Supper. "Yet I am not alone, for the Father is with me."[49] When we lose each other, we still have the journey with God. "I am not alone," I can say too, "for God is with me." But the journey here is essential too, the going on and on, as well as the companionship with God. I think of Robert Burton in his *Anatomy of Melancholy* saying travel is the cure for melancholy, and especially of his final words, "Be not solitary, be not idle."[50] I am not solitary, if I walk alone with God; I am not idle, if I walk on and on.

What then of the sabbath? Is rest in restlessness a way of keeping the sabbath? There is a distinction of times, a differentiation of one time from another in the concept of the sabbath, but there is an integration of times, a unity of all times in the concept of rest in restlessness, an eternity in time. Rest in restlessness turns all of life into a sabbath. Yet all the rhythms of life remain intact, of work and play and repose. So there can be a day of rest even though there is rest also in the restlessness of the other days and there is still the restlessness of the heart that is felt on the day of rest. The attitude carries over from one day to another, though the days differ in their rhythm.

It is an attitude of willingness and hope that allows God to work in my life, to be working still ("My Father is working still, and I work"), a willingness to acknowledge my hunger and thirst, to acknowledge my paralysis and blindness, to acknowledge my mortality, and a hope for the bread and water of life, for healing and the ability to see, for everlasting life. It is a hopeful willingness, a willing hopefulness that is itself an inner peace, a rest in the restless movement of desire toward fulfillment. Is this inner peace itself the bread and water of life, the healing, the ability to see, the everlasting life? It is the spiritual essence, but in the Gospel of John the Word always becomes flesh. There is enough wine at the wedding, enough bread to feed the crowd; the child gets well, the paralyzed man walks, the blind man sees, the dead man lives. Still, it is the spiritual essence that is conveyed by the Word. "It is the spirit that gives life; the flesh is of no avail," Jesus says, after speaking of the bread of life. "The words that I have spoken to you are spirit and life."[51]

All the same, my hope includes the word somehow becoming flesh in my life. "His will is our peace," as Dante says, and the peace of this willingness and hope is an accord with God's will. What is more, "my food is to do the will of him who sent me,"[52] Jesus tells his disciples at the well. It is peace and it is food, and also it is healing and it is life. It is the opposite of the Four Horsemen of the Apocalypse, war and famine and plague and death, and so what Jesus is doing in the Gospels and what God is doing in my life, if I live in the willingness and the hope of the Gospels, is the opposite of what is happening at large in my times, as if God were working upstream, going against the current of human affairs.

Reading the daily newspaper, I find the Four Horsemen of the Apocalypse at work in the world, war and famine and plague and death. Reading the Gospel, I find the opposite at work, peace and sustenance and healing and life. What then of God at work in the world? If God creates by letting be, then I can see how there can be war and famine and plague and death. It is only if we too let be, if we do what God is doing, then there is peace and sustenance and healing and life. One who is detached, who is heart-free, experiences such a joy that no one would be able to take it away, Meister Eckhart says. But such a one remains unsettled. One who has let oneself be, and who has let God be, lives in "wandering joy."[53] I can see the connection between this wandering joy and the happiness Bruce Chatwin finds in wandering peoples. I want to interpret it, though, not as literal wandering from place to place but as a journey in time, a journey with God in time.

To stay in the joy I have to stay on the journey, letting go of things I wanted to be otherwise, praying "Keep me friendly to myself, keep me gentle in disappointment,"[54] for as I meet with disappointment I am tempted to get stuck. I have to go on, therefore, on the Road that goes ever on and on, to take things as meant, knowing the bird cannot fly as long as it is tied by a thread of attachment, to take things as signs when they move in the direction of peace and sustenance and healing and life, to listen to my heart speaking and discern between the journey's direction and that of simple resignation to the inevitable, to know there is a way when there seems to be no way, to know the Road goes ever on when it seems to have come to a dead end. I'm echoing Tolkien here, and I find it helpful to read him when I need to recover my sense of being on a journey.

It is not easy to discern between the journey's direction and that of simple resignation to the inevitable when I try to align the facts of my life with my heart. I suppose the difference is in the element of hope. There is always hope in abandon to the will of God, when "his will is our peace," when I pray "Everything is in your hands," turning over my cares to God. "What may I hope?" Kant's question, goes with his other two questions, "What can I know?" and "What should I do?"[55] Resting in the restless movement of the heart's desire, I am resting in the questions themselves, letting them become prayers like Saint Augustine's questions in his *Confessions,* asking God "What can I know? What should I do? What may I hope?" and then reading the Gospel, letting it speak to my heart. Say I read the story of Jesus healing the paralytic. "Do you want to be healed?"[56] Jesus asks the paralytic. That is the question for me. Or in the King James Version it is "Wilt thou be made whole?" It is a question that speaks to my questions, revealing what I may hope.

"Something we were withholding made us weak," Robert Frost says, "until we found out that it was ourselves we were withholding from our land of living, and forthwith found salvation in surrender."[57] I am like that paralytic. He is withholding something, and I am withholding something, and "it was ourselves we were withholding from our land of living," and for both of us healing or wholeness is in giving ourselves, we find "salvation in surrender." As I ask myself the question "Wilt thou be made whole?" I see the point of Kierkegaard's saying "Purity of heart is to will one thing."[58] For me it is to will the journey with God in time without adding anything, to be willing to walk alone with God, or that is how I describe it to myself in the language of the heart.

"My life is a journey in time, and God is my companion on the way," I began the diary of my first journey by myself through South

America. But I added "Sometimes I wish I had a human companion, visible and tangible." To "will one thing," I see now, I have to drop that addition. All the same, I may be saying something different here than Kierkegaard is saying. For him purity of heart is to will, for me purity of heart is to be willing, to say Yes to Someone or Something. A will to walk alone excludes human companionship. A willingness to walk alone welcomes it. I think of the moment in Tolkien's trilogy when Frodo, the main character, decides he must go on alone into the Land of Shadow, but Sam finds him and insists on coming too. "It is no good trying to escape you," Frodo says. "But I'm glad, Sam. I cannot tell you how glad. Come along! It is plain we were meant to go together."[59] At the very moment he becomes fully willing to walk alone, he finds he has companionship after all.

A woman who recently died, a friend of mine but twenty years younger than I am, appeared to me in a dream, in white dress with bare feet, her face radiant with joy. She called my name, and as I reached to take her hand she turned and then looked back to me as if I were to follow. Then I woke, feeling very happy, as if I had been invited to follow her into paradise, like Dante following Beatrice. I didn't think of it as a call to death so much as a call to discover the realm of eternal life. I think of the concluding words of the Book of Signs, "I know his commandment is eternal life."[60]

If purity of heart is to will one thing, it is to will eternal life. And if purity of heart is not so much to will as to be willing, it is to willingly embrace eternal life. Kierkegaard's will to be oneself is something very lonely, Nietzsche's will to recur eternally is something even more lonely, but a willingness to be oneself, a willingness to embrace eternal life, welcomes company. Can there be company in being oneself, in eternal life? Yes, in being and letting be, in knowing and being known, in loving and being loved. For what is eternal life? All three metaphors of the Gospel of John come into play here, life and light and love. Eternal life is a life that is light, a light that is love. Will goes alone, willingness goes unalone into life and light and love. My dream, my friend inviting me to follow her into paradise, seems to call for a willingness to go unalone into life and light and love. It is true, instead of purity of heart I find in myself a divided heart, a wandering eye, a stifled cry. Still, if I cannot go from there to will one thing, I can go even from there to willingness.

A divided heart, a wandering eye, a stifled cry—it was "something we were withholding" and it was ourselves, "we found out that it was ourselves we were withholding," and so we found "salvation in surrender," not in will but in willingness. At the end of *Repetition,* after having gone through the loss of his beloved Regina, Kierkegaard says "I am again myself."[61] That is the repetition, a return to self. "Keep me friendly to myself" is the key to "keep me gentle in disappointment." If we find "salvation in surrender," however, we find salvation not in getting ourselves back but in being caught up in life and light and love that is greater than ourselves.

"Every one who drinks of this water will thirst again," and so it is with getting ourselves back again, "but whoever drinks of the water that I shall give him will never thirst," and so it is with being caught up in life and light and love that is greater than ourselves, for "the water that I shall give him will become in him a spring of water welling up to eternal life."[62] If I go Kierkegaard's way, receiving myself back after going through loss, like his loss of Regina, I will thirst again. If I go Dante's way, if I follow my dream, following my friend as she leads me into paradise, like Dante following Beatrice, I will never thirst, I will find "a spring of water welling up to eternal life." Here I find myself reading not just the gospel but *The Divine Comedy,* actually reading Helen Luke's commentary, *Dark Wood to White Rose,* and trying to find my own way from the dark wood to the white rose. "See what I am,"[63] Beatrice says to Dante, and her smile becomes ever more joyous as he ascends into paradise. I think of the radiant smile of my friend in my dream.

If the love of God is simply joy at the thought of God, as Spinoza says, then following this joy is being led by the love of God, being caught up in "the love that moves the sun and the other stars,"[64] as

Dante says in the last line of *Paradiso*. It is joy at the thought of "God for us," as my friend used to say, at the thought of "God in communion with us."[65] For me it is joy simply at the thought of being on a journey with God in time. That for me is the love of God. It is the life that is light, the light that is love.

"Heart Always Contemplating Communion"

There is an edge of vision here. Dante's white rose is beyond the edge of the visible universe, the event horizon as we call it nowadays. It is when the joy carries him beyond the edge of vision that he finds the love that moves the sun and the stars. So too in the Gospel of John, "Lord, show us the Father, and we shall be satisfied," Philip says to Jesus at the Last Supper. And Jesus replies "Have I been with you so long, and yet you do not know me, Philip? He who has seen me has seen the Father. . . ."[66] One who sees what Jesus is doing sees what God is doing, but it takes faith to see God in him. "Faith is God sensible to the heart,"[67] as Pascal says. If my life is a journey in time, God is "sensible to the heart" on my way, and it is only with the heart that I can see beyond the event horizon.

There is an event horizon of my life, just as there is of the visible universe, and it is time, my journey is in time, and in the prologue of *Being and Time* Heidegger speaks of "*time* as the possible horizon for any understanding whatsoever of being."[68] Yet there is something timeless as well, "the singing timelessness of the heart,"[69] as Broch calls it in *The Death of Virgil,* and it is the singing timelessness of the heart that is able to follow, like Dante following Beatrice, into the realm of eternal life. There is an inner peace that is the necessary and sufficient condition for this singing timelessness. "My soul was not still enough for songs," MacDonald says at one point in *Phantastes.* "Only in the silence and darkness of the soul's night do those stars of the inward firmament sink to its lower surface from the singing realms beyond, and shine upon the conscious spirit."[70] When I am not at peace, when I wake up troubled in the middle of the night, I have first to calm myself and come again to peace in God's will.

But what is God's will? Is it to let go of earthly ties, as the bird cannot fly as long as it is held by a thread? I had thought of life as a journey *with God* and *in time,* but to follow into eternal life like Dante following Beatrice would be a journey *to God* and *into eternity.* "Where I am going you cannot come" Jesus tells his disciples at the Last Supper, and that seems to preclude such a journey, but then he goes on to say "Let not your hearts be troubled. . . . In my Father's house are many rooms . . . and when I go and prepare a place for you, I will come again and will take you to myself, that where I am you may be also."[71] I am to continue with God and in time, I gather, and the journey will lead to God and into eternity. To follow my friend into paradise is simply to follow joy, I gather, the joy of "God with us," to live in the peace, the peace of "his will is our peace."

"I am with you." That is what my friend Henri Nouwen called "the inner voice of love,"[72] describing his recovery from a breakdown late in his life due to the loss of a friendship. That is the voice I hear in the last discourses of Jesus in the Gospel of John (chapters 13–17). There are "three voices of poetry,"[73] according to T. S. Eliot, the first the solitary voice of the One, the second the voice of the One before the Many, and the third the manifold voice of the Many. As I read the last discourses, they are in the third voice when the disciples pose questions to Jesus, in the second when he teaches them, and in the first when he prays at the end.

There are two great questions in the Gospel of John, "Where do you come from?" and "Where are you going?" and it is especially this second one that the disciples are asking at the Last Supper. If I ask myself these questions and if I think of the old man saying to Lawrence of Arabia, "The love is from God and of God and towards God," I begin to understand what Jesus is saying in these last discourses: the life, the light, the love is from God and of God and towards God. Or, moving from the third person to the first person, I hear him saying I am from God and of God and towards God, and then moving from the first person to the second person, I hear him saying you are from God and of God and towards God, what is true of me comes to be true also of you who believe in me, and it comes true of you in and only in relation to me. Where then do you come from? Not just from this world but from God. Where then are you going? To God, to be with me, God in me and I in you.

"Heart always contemplating communion," that seems the essence of these last discourses. That is the motto of a friend who is a bishop in Bangladesh, Patrick D'Rosario of Chittagong. In Bengali it is *milon shadhonay mogno antore,* an open-ended saying, my friend tells me, and difficult to translate, though this is his translation, "heart always contemplating communion."[74] In these last discourses it is the heart of Jesus always contemplating communion with God and communion with his disciples. If I move into that stance myself, my own heart always contemplating communion, I come into touch with my own loneliness, my own longing for communion, and I wonder if the communion spoken of in these discourses is enough for me.

There is reassurance in the words, "These things I have spoken unto you, that my joy might remain in you, and that your joy might be full."[75] These words, "that my joy might remain," are the title of a novel in French by Jean Giono, *Que ma Joie Demeure.* In the English translation it is called, like the Bach Cantata, *Joy of Man's Desiring.* The joy that remains is indeed the joy of our desiring. Giono's vision here, as in his little story *The Man Who Planted Trees,* is of a "man who planted hope and grew happiness."[76] That is what Jesus is in these last discourses, "the man who planted hope and grew happiness." What is the hope? It is like the motto, "heart always contemplating communion," open-ended. It is communion that is the joy of our desiring, communion with one another, in Giono's vision by way of communion with nature, in the Gospel of John by way of communion with God, "I in them and thou in me."[77]

There is the key, not simply "I and thou" with one another or "I and thou" with nature, but "I in them and thou in me." My journey with God in time is a journey with God who is "God with us," Emmanuel, and so is a version of "I in them and thou in me," where "I" is the "I am" of Christ, and "thou" is the God he calls Abba, and "them" are "those whom thou hast given me." That sounds complex, but there is a simplicity here in that preposition "in" and in the thought of indwelling. The metaphor here is one of dwelling and indwelling, whereas the metaphor I am using is one of traveling, a journey with God in time. The metaphor of traveling is there in the Gospel of John in the two great questions "Where do you come from?" and "Where are you going?" If I translate also the metaphor of indwelling into that of travel, I get something like a journey with God in time.

What is God in the Gospel of John? And what is a journey from God and to God, what I am calling a journey with God? "God is spirit" in the Gospel and "God is light" and "God is love"[78] in the First Epistle of John. I think again of the three great metaphors, life and light and love. A journey from God and to God, a journey with God who is spirit, who is light, who is love, is a life in time directed by the illumining of the mind and the kindling of the heart. "We are to do nothing but wait," Heidegger's saying on thinking, we could apply here, saying we are to do nothing but wait on the kindling of the heart and the illumining of the mind. That is different than waiting on events, waiting for something to happen outside of ourselves, waiting, for instance, for someone to come into my life or for someone to come back into my life. It is instead waiting on the movement of spirit, on the movement of love, on the illumining and the kindling that takes place in my own mind and heart, and envisioning action based on the illumining spirit and the kindling love. It is waiting on God, *attente de Dieu*, as Simone Weil says, paying attention to God, rather than "waiting for Godot,"[79] waiting for something to happen.

If I pay attention, I become aware of an inner light enlightening, guiding, assuring me, not that I see the light itself but I see things in the light. Here is my joy, unfelt when I am not paying attention, caught up in the sadness of the parting of friends. This is the Comforter that Jesus speaks of in these last discourses, the Counselor. "Attention is the natural prayer of the soul," and if I pray, letting the inner light enlighten and guide and assure me, my prayer becomes like that of Jesus at the end of these discourses, a kind of distillation of the Lord's Prayer given in Matthew and Luke, "I in them and thou in me," where "I" now is my own "I am" and "thou" is "God with us" and "them" are "those whom thou hast given me," all the persons who belong to my life.

It is possible to be guided and yet be unaware that one is being guided. "Day after day he held on, and he thought he had no guide," it is said in *The Golden Key.* "He did not see how a shining fish under the waters directed his steps."[80] So it is too with being enlightened and being assured. There is an enlightenment in the simplicity of this vision of a journey with God in time. I become aware of the enlightenment when I become aware of "the simplicity of vision,"[81] how it unifies my life. Moreover, there is a guidance in the step by step of insight by insight, for instance as I write these paragraphs, day by day, passing from sadness to joy as I pay attention. And there is an assurance of "I am with you" as I become aware of "the simplicity of vision" and I realize it is true also of me to say "a shining fish under the waters directed his steps." There is joy in becoming aware like this of the inner light, the joyful thought of God that Spinoza calls the love of God.

Where the difficulty lies is in the spiritual quality of all this, "God is spirit" and "It is the spirit that gives life, the flesh is of no avail" and "the words that I have spoken to you are spirit and life." There is a desolation of spirit I experience when my own orientation is not spiritual, when I live with a divided heart, a wandering eye, a stifled cry. A spiritual orientation like Kierkegaard's "purity of heart is to will one thing," for me a willingness rather than a will, is a Yes to the God who is spirit, to the spirit that gives life, to the words that are spirit and life. It is essentially a willingness to follow the inner light.

To say "God is spirit" in the language of the Gospel of John is to say "God is life" but "life" here is eternal life as in "spirit and life" and "it is the spirit that gives life," and the sentence is like "God is light" and "God is love" in the epistle, God is the life that is light, the light that is love. If I may interpret the three great metaphors here in terms of the inner light, I can say the light answers to my divided heart, my wandering eye, my stifled cry. A divided heart is a complexity of life, as a life is said to become complicated when there is some new involvement with another person. The enlightenment that comes of the inner light, on the other hand, is "the simplicity of vision," a simplification of life around a vision like that of a journey with God. A wandering eye is a disorientation arising out of the restless movement of loneliness, always looking for someone to make me unalone. The guidance that comes of the inner light, on the other hand, is a regaining of perspective, of letting be and being open to the mystery of encounter. A stifled cry is a cry of loneliness, a cry for love, unexpressed because there seems no way of answering it. The assurance that comes of the inner light, on the other hand, meets the cry with "the inner voice of love," the sense of "I am with you."

Just as the Lord's Prayer in Matthew and Luke is a summary of the teaching of Jesus, so the prayer here in John is a summary of these last discourses, "heart always contemplating communion." If I read these discourses in the inner light, I encounter what is called "the hermeneutic circle,"[82] I see the discourses in terms of the light and vice-versa I see the light in terms of the discourses, and thus there is a circle in my thinking. I can see the loneliness I bring to this in my divided heart and wandering eye and stifled cry, and I can hope that the hermeneutic circle, as Heidegger argues, is not a vicious circle, and so I am actually finding here an answer to loneliness.

What then is the answer to loneliness? It is the God who is life and light and love. Whenever you make a statement about God, you get far-reaching consequences, for instance think of Einstein's saying, "God does not play dice" (*Gott würfelt nicht*). So if I say "God is life and light and love," understanding these metaphors as they are used in the Gospel of John, this has far-reaching consequences for my notion of life as a journey with God in time. I am seeing my life as a journey with the God who is life and light and love. "One who follows me will not walk in darkness,"[83] Jesus says in John, and those are the opening words of *The Imitation of Christ*. If I interpret life and light and love in terms of the inner light, and if I call the inner light not only the Light Within but the Christ Within, as the Quakers do, then to follow Christ is to follow the inner light. And if I follow the light, I will not walk in the dark of loneliness. I take that to mean the light will shine even in the dark of loneliness. Although I am lonely, my loneliness will not overshadow the divine presence.

Here I am echoing the prologue,

> and the light shines in the darkness,
> and the darkness has not overshadowed it.

I suppose it is essential to answer loneliness and to answer it with divine presence, "God with us." If loneliness is not answered and cannot be answered, if "God is dead" and we are nevertheless in touch with the heart, like Nietzsche, then we have "heart always contemplating communion" but in vain. "And when you look long into an abyss," Nietzsche says, "the abyss also looks into you."[84] So it is with loneliness; so it is also with communion. In fact, it is the longing in the loneliness that becomes the love, I believe, the love that is from God and of God and towards God.

"One who loves God cannot endeavour to bring it about that God should love him in return," Spinoza says, and yet "The mind's intellectual love of God is the very love of God with which God loves himself."[85] God in the Gospel of John takes the initiative in love, and so it is we who love in return, but there too the love of God is God's own love. I am caught up then in the love that comes from God and goes to God, in a to-and-fro with God, when I love God, when I feel joy at the thought of being on a journey with God. "I came from the Father and have come into the world; again I am leaving the world and going to the Father,"[86] Jesus says in conclusion at the Last Supper, ascribing to himself what can be said of the love that comes from God and goes to God. "I come from God and have come into the world; again I am leaving the world and going to God" I can say too to the extent that I am caught up in the love of God, to the extent that "I in them and thou in me" comes true in my life and I follow the inner light, the Christ Within. I feel here an answer to loneliness, being caught up in something greater than myself. The answer depends on becoming, as Novalis described Spinoza, "a man inebriated with God,"[87] in love with God.

All this goes back to something very primordial and elemental, something that encompasses life and death, "Enoch walked with God; then he was no more, because God took him."[88] Once upon a time, according to storytelling, we walked with God and we knew "the language of the birds"[89] and of other living beings. Then came a second age when the human race emerged and separated from other living beings and even from God, then a third age, our own, in which the individual emerged and separated from humanity, thus the terrible loneliness we experience. Beyond this a fourth age can be envisioned in which we are reunited with God and with one another, and that seems to be the vision of the Gospel of John, "I in them and thou in me." It is the vision of the "heart always contemplating communion."

A road opens up in this vision, "the road of the union of love with God,"[90] as it is called in *The Dark Night of the Soul*, the road of reunion with God and humanity, the road of my journey with God in time. The "dark night" for me is the night of loneliness, and I am guided by the inner light, as in the mystical poem Dark Night,

> In the lucky night,
> in secret so nobody saw me
> and I saw no thing,
> with no light no guide other
> than that burning in my heart.[91]

It is "the lucky night" (*la noche dichosa*) of loneliness, as I understand it, because the longing in the loneliness becomes the love.

Have I gotten into something foreign here to the Gospel of John? No, I think not, for the three great metaphors of life and light and love are related somehow to their opposites, death and darkness and lovelessness, and there is a way from death to life, from darkness to light, from lovelessness to love, and that way is indeed "the road of the union of love with God."

"Lord, we do not know where you are going; how can we know the way?" Thomas asks at the Last Supper. "I am the way, and the truth, and the life," Jesus replies; "no one comes to the Father, but by me."[92] The incarnation, the Word become flesh, is where the opposites meet, where death meets life, where darkness meets light, where lovelessness meets love. And so Jesus himself, the Word become flesh, is the way from death to life, from darkness to light, from lovelessness to love. How? By entering into his relation with God. If I enter into his relation with God, the God he calls Abba, if I make his God my God, then I live in him and he lives in me, "Abide in me, and I in you."[93] The relation of Jesus with God, his "I and thou" with God, is "unconditional relation," as Martin Buber calls it in *I and Thou,* and the Gospel of John, as he says, is "the Gospel of pure relation."[94] Let us see what it would be to enter into pure relation and so to pass from the loneliness to the love.

The Way of Pure Relation

When Jesus says *I* "it is the *I* of unconditional relation," Martin Buber says, "in which the man calls his *thou* Father in such a way that he himself is simply Son, and nothing else but Son."[95] Unconditional relation thus means living entirely in relation. "Every one can say *thou* and is then *I,*" Buber goes on to say, "every one can say Father and is then Son." So there is something universal here, something that can come true in every life. Where what Buber is saying from a Jewish standpoint differs from the Gospel of John, it seems to me, can be seen in the two formulas, Buber's "I and thou" and John's "I in them and thou in me." What John's formula adds is the note of indwelling, God dwelling in Christ ("thou in me") and Christ dwelling in us ("I in them"). Loneliness, the longing to be unalone, is met in "I in them and thou in me" in a way it cannot be met simply in "I and thou."

Indwelling is linked with the death and resurrection of Jesus, with Jesus being alive and living in us. There is an indwelling in knowing insofar as "we can know more than we can tell," a dwelling in the particulars of what we know. I can know more than I can tell of another person, dwelling in the particulars of our relationship, the ins and outs of our dealings with one another, and I can know more than I can tell of God, dwelling in the particulars of my relationship with God, my experience of prayers answered and unanswered. So if I enter into the relation of Jesus with God, saying for instance the Lord's Prayer, I dwell in the particulars of his relation with God, the name, the kingdom, the will, the bread, the forgiveness, the guiding and guarding from temptation and evil. Or in terms of the Gospel of John, I dwell in the sense of coming from God and going to God, in the sense of life and light and love. As I dwell in life and light and love, I dwell in him and he dwells in me.

It is only after his death that indwelling becomes possible, "unless the grain of wheat falls into the earth and dies, it remains alone; but if it dies, it bears much fruit."[96] When a friend dies, the "I and thou" of our friendship remains but the "it" is taken away, what we had together is gone. The "I and thou" then becomes "pure relation" and things are possible which were impossible when we were both alive. I think again of my dream in which a friend appeared right after her death and seemed to invite me to follow her, like Dante following Beatrice into paradise. "It is to your advantage that I go away," Jesus tells his disciples at the Last Supper, "for if I do not go away, the Counselor will not come to you; but if I go, I will send him to you."[97] The term Paraclete is translated Counselor in the Revised Standard Version and Comforter in the King James Version. The Spirit that was in Jesus passes into his disciples after his death and this Spirit then becomes his indwelling presence in them, "I in them," the Counselor in them, the Comforter in them.

There is a paradox, nevertheless, in the death of Jesus on the cross, and the way of pure relation here becomes a way of paradox: the shame of the cross is called "glory" and the lifting up on the cross is a lifting up in glory, "and I, when I am lifted up from the earth, will draw all to myself."[98] Here is where death meets life, and darkness meets light, and lovelessness meets love. Here is where God is revealed as life and light and love. How am I to follow on this way?

If I am to dwell in the particulars of his relation with God, if I am to dwell in life and light and love, I have to relate somehow to the opposites, to death and darkness and lovelessness. So in my life too death will meet life and darkness will meet light and lovelessness will meet love. How? That is "the mystery of encounter" and is different in every life. The real question here is about God. Is there a dark side of God encompassing death and darkness and lovelessness, as Jung says in *Answer to Job*?[99] Or is it, as John says in his Epistle, "God is light and in him is no darkness at all"?[100] I am reading John here and I want to go with his sense of a God who is life and light and love. More than that, I want to enter into the relation of Jesus with God, to trust God as he did, calling God Abba. It is one thing, though, to say there is no death, no darkness, no lovelessness in God, but another to say there is a relation to death, to darkness, to lovelessness, as in the sentence of the prologue, "and the light shines in the darkness, and the darkness has not overshadowed it." That is what I want to say. God is life and light and love, but in the Word made flesh death meets life, and darkness meets light, and lovelessness meets love. Therefore the cross.

"Now is my soul troubled. And what shall I say? Father, save me from this hour? No, for this purpose I have come to this hour. Father, glorify thy name," Jesus prays in John. "Then a voice came from heaven, I have glorified it, and I will glorify it again."[101] That is all there is left of the conflict of wills, of his wrestling with God in the Gospel of John, only a vestige of the agony in the garden re-counted in Matthew and Mark and Luke. It is the conflict you feel when your prayers are not answered or when God, instead of ful-filling your wishes, simply answers "I am with you." There is a deep mystery of encounter here, how death meeting life, darkness meeting light, lovelessness meeting love, can glorify the name of the Father, can show Jesus to be the Son of God, as the centurion says who sees Jesus die, "Truly this man was the Son of God!"[102]

What is the mystery of encounter? Is it this encounter with God in prayer, or is it the encounter with human beings or with human situations? "Our relation to our fellow human beings is that of prayer," Kafka says, "our relation to ourselves, that of striv-ing."[103] I have taken this phrase "the mystery of encounter" from Paul Celan. "The poem is lonely. It is lonely and *en route*. Its au-thor stays with it," Celan says."Does this very fact not place the poem already here, at its inception, in the encounter, *in the mys-tery of encounter?*"[104] So it is with life in this third age. The life of the emerged and separated individual is lonely. It is lonely and *en route,* a journey in time. The individual stays with it, like the au-thor with a poem. And does this very fact not place the life of the individual too, at its inception, in the encounter, in the mystery of encounter ? If I think of my life as a journey with God in time, en-counter seems significant, seems indeed to be mystery pregnant with meaning. And if "attention is the natural prayer of the soul," it is above all attention to the mystery of encounter. Where does all this leave me, though, when things fall apart, when human re-lations fall apart? Indwelling seems the answer, "Abide in me, and I in you."

Dwelling in the particulars of a relation, I am dwelling in a re-lation to particulars. I find I don't have to take the particulars of my life as the will of God for me but to look for the divine will rather in my relation to the particulars, in letting them be and being open to the mystery that shows itself and withdraws in them. When things fall apart, for instance, I don't have to tell my-self it is the will of God for me that things fall apart, but I look for

God rather in the kindling of my heart and the illumining of my mind in the face of things falling apart. Here too "God is spirit" and "God is light" and "God is love" and God is to be found in the illumining of the mind and the kindling of the heart rather than in things falling apart. God's will for me, then, is in the willingness and hope inspired by the kindling and illumining, in my release-ment of mind and heart towards things. For the will of God in the Gospel of John is seen as what God commands, not simply as what happens, "and I know that his commandment is eternal life." This can lead, I gather, to an attitude of releasement towards what happens, for instance to things falling apart.

Here I am using Meister Eckhart's idea of "releasement toward things" *(Die Gelassenheit zu den Dingen),* revived in our times by Heidegger. If we interpret the Gospel of John as "the Gospel of pure relation" and try to live the Gospel, we are left with a residue of things, what to do about things, the things spoken of in the prologue, "all came to be through this, and without this nothing came that ever came to be." Letting be, it seems, is doing what God is doing, "Let there be light," and seems to go with Jesus healing on the sabbath, doing what God is doing, as if God were still creating and had not come yet to the eternal sabbath of rest. Letting be is a comportment towards things, Heidegger says, "which expresses Yes and at the same time No."[105] It is a Yes to things, even to things falling apart, but also a No in that its Yes is to the relation more than to the things. Thus "his will is our peace" comes true here in letting be, more than in things falling apart. This can seem a rather subtle distinction, but it is the difference between faith and infinite resignation.

"What seems easier than to let a being be just the being that it is?" Heidegger asks. "Or does this turn out to be the most difficult of tasks, particularly if such a project—to let a being be as it is—represents the opposite of the indifference that simply turns its back on the being itself?"[106] I apply this to human relations, letting another person be, without turning my back on the person, and I think I have found a kind of detachment in love, a detachment that is not just infinite resignation, a realization that the other person is beyond my control, but a detachment in love, a detachment in faith that does not give up hope of reunion, a turning toward rather than a turning away. Maybe letting be like this is not only the essence of being, as Heidegger suggests, but also the essence of love.

"Releasement toward things and openness to the mystery belong together,"[107] and so it is here as well. There is the mystery I encounter in God when my prayers go unanswered or when God answers with "I am with you" instead of fulfilling my wishes, and there is the mystery I encounter in human beings that "shows itself and at the same time withdraws"[108] when they withdraw, when a friend withdraws from my life. What these instances seem to have in common is that I encounter something that is against my own will. What answer do I find in the Gospel of John? The divine will, according to John, is a will to eternal life, "and I know that his commandment is eternal life." There is "a breath of eternal life,"[109] according to Buber, in the human "I and thou." I take it this breath of eternal life is the element of God's will, the eternal element in a human relation. The "it" in a human relation, on the other hand, the thing we have together, is the ephemeral element, the thing that passes when contact is broken off by death or by choice or by circumstance. As when a friend dies, so when a friend withdraws from my life, I lose the "it" of our relation, but the "I and thou" can survive, can even be a mutual relation.

"We can have abundant life even though many wishes remain unfulfilled,"[110] Dietrich Bonhoeffer observed when he was in prison (for the plot to kill Hitler) and many of his own wishes were unfulfilled. I see an answer in this as to why many prayers are unanswered or are answered only with "I am with you." If the will of God is eternal life or "abundant life," as in the saying "I came that they may have life, and have it abundantly,"[111] then I can see how many wishes fall outside the will of God. Also I can see how my wish to recover the "it" of our relationship, when I have lost a friend, can go unfulfilled and my prayers be unanswered when I appeal to God. I can see how God, whose will for me is abundant life, can answer my prayers simply with "I am with you."

What then is abundant life? I think of a little church I once saw with a sign in front reading

Abundant Life Fellowship
Welcome

As I read the beginning of John's First Epistle, I find this language of fellowship (*koinonia*), "that which we have seen and heard we proclaim also to you, so that you may have fellowship with us; and our fellowship is with the Father and with his Son Jesus Christ" and "that your joy may be full."[112] Or instead of "fellowship" we could translate "communion." At any rate the idea is the same as "I in them and thou in me" or "And this is eternal life, that they may know thee the only true God, and Jesus Christ whom thou hast sent."[113] Knowing God and knowing Christ is knowing by indwelling as in "we can know more than we can tell," and the indwelling, "I in them and thou in me," is what constitutes the abundant life fellowship or the abundant life communion. Is this the answer to my loneliness?

Not if I take it to mean simply belonging, though that is a basic human need, the need to belong. No, it answers loneliness only if I take it to mean indwelling. There is a poem about indwelling in Heidegger's "Conversation on a Country Path":

In-dwelling

Never one truth alone;
To receive intact
The coming forth of truth's nature
In return for boundless steadfastness:
Imbed the thinking heart
In the humble patience
Of unique high-minded
And noble memories.[114]

There the conversation is about indwelling in releasement, in letting be (*Gelassenheit*). Here in speaking of "I in them and thou in me," we are speaking of indwelling in the particulars of a relation with God, but if God does indeed create by letting be, as in "Let there be light," then here too we are dwelling in releasement.

"Never one truth alone"—there is never just the truth of my own life, but there is always the truth also of the real presences in my life, the truth above all of Someone or Something greater than myself present in me. "Attention is the natural prayer of the soul" and so "to receive intact the coming forth of truth's nature in return for boundless steadfastness" I have to "imbed the thinking heart in the humble patience of unique high-minded and noble memories." Waiting on God to lead me by kindling my heart and illumining my mind, I come to something like the stance Dag Hammarskjöld comes to in his diary *Markings,* "For all that has been—Thanks! To all that shall be—Yes!"[115] I do indeed have to "imbed the thinking heart in the humble patience of unique high-minded and noble memories" in order to say "For all that has been—Thanks!" And "to receive intact the coming forth of truth's nature in return for boundless steadfastness" I have to be able to say "To all that shall be—Yes!"

"Thanks!" and "Yes!" is a lonely man's answer ("loneliness" is perhaps the most frequent noun in *Markings*), and it can seem to imply that whatever happens is the will of God, but actually the "Thanks!" and "Yes!" is to events as seen in the inner light, and so really it is "Thanks!" and "Yes!" to life and light and love. It is a lonely man's answer. "The hour is coming, indeed it has come, when you will be scattered, every man to his home, and will leave me alone," Jesus says at the Last Supper, "yet I am not alone, for the Father is with me." For if I say "Thanks!" and "Yes!" like this, my life does become a journey with God in time, and so I am unalone even when I am most alone.

That parable of Saint John of the Cross does hold true, a bird cannot fly as long as it is tied only by a thread.[116] I break the thread of attachment as I say "Thanks!" and "Yes!" It is clear, the Gospel of John invites me to life and light and love and "we can have abundant life even though many wishes remain unfulfilled." Now I am reluctantly seeing this means "letting self-will go in favor of the divine will,"[117] the very thing Heidegger did not want to accept in taking over the idea of releasement or letting be (*Gelassenheit*) from Meister Eckhart. Also, as I cite the mystics, Meister Eckhart and Saint John of the Cross, I realize I am speaking of "a mystical relation" with Jesus and with God, the very thing Rudolf Bultmann denies in his interpretation of the Gospel of John. As I see it, I enter into the mystical relation "I in them and thou in me" as I say "Thanks!" and "Yes!" letting go of self-will, my many unfulfilled wishes, in favor of the divine will to life and light and love.

I said "reluctantly." How am I to get past my reluctance in letting go of self-will in favor of the divine will? The letting go is there in the "Thanks!" and "Yes!" "I have come down from heaven, not to do my own will but the will of him who sent me,"[118] the saying of Jesus applies to me too in following him. My "Thanks!" is a letting go of "all that has been," seeing it as the journey behind me. My "Yes!" then is an openness to the mystery of "all that shall be," seeing it as the journey ahead of me. "The simplicity of vision" that I find in the thought of a journey with God in time makes it possible for me to put my heart into my "Thanks!" and my "Yes!"

Indwelling is "not a mystical relation between Jesus and his own," Bultmann says, "only in faith is this existence a reality—*not in any direct relationship to Jesus or to God.*"[119] As I see it, though, faith is reliance on God, leaning on God for support, and we experience not only the leaning, the believing, but also the support, the presence of God. So indwelling is an experience, though it depends on faith. So too it makes sense to say we know God and we know Christ, knowing by indwelling, as "we can know more than we can tell," though the knowing comes of believing. So it seems to me *we do have a direct relationship to Jesus and to God,* "I and thou" or "I in them and thou in me," though "only in faith is this existence a reality." The relation between Jesus and his own thus is indeed "a mystical relation" in John, though it is, as in Paul, "that Christ may dwell in your hearts through faith."[120]

It is in faith then that I say "Thanks!" thinking of the road behind, and "Yes!" thinking of the road ahead. It does take faith to say "Thanks!" and "Yes!" when I think of loss. (Today I visited a friend who has lost her eyesight.) It is true, "thinking is thanking," the mystic saying that Heidegger always quotes, can be said without faith, as he says it, "of that thanking which does not have to thank for something, but only thanks for being allowed to thank."[121] "Yes" too can be said without faith, like Nietzsche's "Yes." What faith adds to willingness is hope, the hope I suppose of abundant life. Even if many wishes remain unfulfilled, I can hope to have life and have it abundantly. But hoping and relying on God for it, I can actually live it, even in a very restrictive situation, like Bonhoeffer in prison. That is what I find, reading the Gospel of John, abundant life.

Hoping and relying on God for abundant life and thinking of my friend who has lost her eyesight and of a dream-vision she had of a little girl putting her hand into the hand of God, I think of the poem of M. L. Haskins quoted by George VI in the dark days of 1939,

> And I said to the man who stood at the gate of the
> year, Give me a light that I may tread safely into the
> unknown. And he replied, Go out into the darkness
> and put your hand into the hand of God. That shall
> be to you better than light and safer than a known way.[122]

The light that shines in the darkness can seem dark to me, like all light passing through darkness, until I put my trust in it and let it illumine my way. When I put my hand into the hand of God, I walk with God in life and light and love.

Parables

*Why such reluctance? If you only
followed the parables you yourselves
would become parables and with that
rid of all your daily cares.*

—Franz Kafka

My stomach roils at the thought of my life becoming complicated with affairs. When I think of my life as a journey with God in time, though, peace returns. That is a sign that even my body wants "the simplicity of vision." I seem to find that simplicity in sayings and stories, as my philosopher friend Martin Versfeld did in later life, especially in the sayings and stories of the Gospel.

It is as if a journey with God in time were a parable, not itself one of the parables of Jesus, but one that comes into being when we follow his parables, for instance when I follow his Parable of the Sower and go out myself to sow the seed that is the word of God. "Why such reluctance?" Kafka says to those who don't take parables seriously, setting parables against the reality of our daily cares. "If you only followed the parables," he says, "you yourselves would become parables and with that rid of all your daily cares." Then a little exchange follows:

Q. I bet that is also a parable.
A. You have won.
Q. But unfortunately only in parable.
A. No, in reality: in parable you have lost.[1]

So this saying of Kafka's is a parable about parables. Let us apply it to the parables of Jesus. If we follow the parables, do we become parables ourselves and thereby heart-free? Do we find ourselves on a journey with God in time?

A journey is a lived parable. What then is a parable? The word *parabole* in Greek, the word that is used in Matthew and Mark and Luke, means a juxtaposition, a comparison, especially in the form of a brief story. The word *paroimia* is used in John and means a figure or a proverb. When Jesus speaks openly at last in John and without figures, he uses the language of the journey. "I came from the Father and have come into the world," he says; "again, I am leaving the world and going to the Father," and his disciples say "Ah, now you are speaking plainly, not in any figure!"[2] But is he speaking plainly, and not in any figure? We could have the same exchange with him that Kafka has, "I bet that is also a parable. You have won. But unfortunately only in parable. No, in reality: in parable you have lost." There are two sayings of Jesus that are generally known among Muslims, one the well-known saying from Matthew and Luke, "Foxes have holes and birds of the air have nests; but the Son of Man has nowhere to lay his head," the other a saying not found in the Gospels, "This world is a bridge: pass over it, but do not build your house on it."[3] Both of them speak of life as a journey and point to the parable we become if we follow Christ.

"Many complain that the words of the wise are always merely parables and of no use in daily life, which is the only life we have," Kafka says. "When the sage says: *Go over,* he does not mean that we should cross to some actual place, which we could do anyhow if the labor were worth it; he means some fabulous yonder, something unknown to us, something too that he cannot designate more precisely and therefore cannot help us here in the very least."[4] The parables of Jesus too seem to be saying something like *Go over*, if I am reading them rightly, "This world is a bridge: pass over it, but do not build your house on it." Let us see if Kafka's own answer works here, if we only followed the parables we ourselves would become parables and would be heart-free of our daily cares.

The Secrets of the Kingdom

Go over. Passing over here is like all passing over, it is followed by coming back. If I pass over into the Parable of the Sower, I pass over into the figure of the Sower who sows the seed broadcast, some falling on the path, some on rocky ground, some among thorns, and some on fertile ground.[5] I think of my own experience of teaching, how my students come to my words with many different frames of mind, some more, some less receptive. Coming back to myself, I realize I am like the Sower who sows the word of teaching broadcast among his listeners, that my task is just that, to broadcast the word of teaching, "broadcast" here being used in its old sense before radio to mean casting abroad, the arm motion of the Sower broadcasting the seed. At the same time I realize I have no control over the ground on which the seed falls, no control over the results of my teaching. I have to let go of the seed as I broadcast it, to let my listeners be, to let them be as receptive or unreceptive as they are. If I follow, then, the Parable of the Sower, I myself become a parable, I become a sower, and I become heart-free, letting go of the seed as I broadcast it, letting my listeners listen as they will.

So the parable goes in Matthew and Mark and Luke, but in John there is more, there is what we might call the Parable of the Reaper and there is the saying, "One sows and another reaps."[6] How am I to follow this parable? "I have sent you to reap that for which you did not labor; others have labored, and you have entered into their labors," Jesus says in John, and "The harvest is plentiful, but the laborers are few," he says in Matthew and Luke.[7] I take it that those who listen to me are "those whom thou hast given me" in the language of John. So my teaching them, though from one standpoint it is sowing, from another is reaping, and reaping what I have not sown. So insofar as I become a parable here, I become a reaper, and I become still more heart-free, letting go of credit for my listeners and taking them instead as a gift given to me.

There are other parables that are extensions of the Parable of the Sower, namely that of the Seed Growing Secretly, that of the Mustard Seed, and that of the Weeds, but according to Mark the Parable of the Sower is The Parable. "Do you not understand this parable?" Jesus asks in Mark. "How then will you understand all the parables?"[8] Have I understood this parable? Why do I identify with the Sower? Why do I not ask myself instead what sort of ground I am for the seed, fertile or infertile? I suppose it is because of my loneliness, wanting to be understood by others. The Parable of the Sower speaks strongly to my loneliness, calling on me to let go of the demand to be understood and to receive whatever understanding I do receive as a gift. I see this longing to be understood in the teachings and parables of Jesus, especially in Mark, where Jesus is seen, as the story goes on, becoming more and more alone. On the other hand, there is an equal and opposite desire for secrecy that appears as well. "To you has been given the secret of the kingdom of God," Jesus says to his disciples in Mark, "but for those outside everything is in parables; so that they may indeed see but not perceive, and may indeed hear but not understand."[9]

Let us see if we can understand "the genesis of secrecy"[10] here, as it is called. I see a parallel between "the secret of the kingdom of God," as Mark calls it, "the secrets of the kingdom of heaven," as Matthew calls them, "the secrets of the kingdom of God," as Luke calls them, and what the mystics call "the secrets of love."[11] This last is a phrase that Ramon Lull uses in *The Book of the Lover and the Beloved*. I once looked up the original Catalan of Lull's work and found the word for "secrets" is *secrets!*

There is a secrecy about the secrets of love that is not taken away even when they are revealed, "for secretly the Lover hides the secrets of his Beloved," Lull says, "secretly also he reveals them, and yet when they are revealed he keeps them secret still."[12] As I understand this, the secrets of love remain secret even when they are revealed, except to one who loves. One who does not love does not understand the secrets even when they are revealed. I find something similar to this in the Gospel of John. "Lord, how is it that you will manifest yourself to us, and not to the world?" Judas (not the Iscariot) asks Jesus at the Last Supper. "If a man loves me, he will keep my word, and my Father will love him, and we will come to him and make our home with him," Jesus replies. "He who does not love me does not keep my words; and the word which you hear is not mine but the Father's who sent me."[13] So the secrets of the kingdom remain secret even when they are revealed, except to those who love him and keep his words. Only those who love can understand.

What are the secrets? There is a knowing that comes of loving, specifically a knowing that comes of loving God, and that knowing, *gnosis* as it is called in *The Gospel of Truth,* amounts to *knowing the loving God.* Here I realize I am citing a Gnostic text, but there is a remarkably clear insight there into "the secrets of the kingdom" as they are called in the canonical Gospels. "The gospel of truth is joy for those who have received from the Father of truth the grace of knowing him, through the power of the Word," it begins, and then further on, "ignorance of the Father brought about anguish and terror" and further "Since oblivion came into existence because the Father was not known, then if the Father comes to be known, oblivion will not exist from that moment on."[14] Anguish and terror come of not knowing the loving God, I gather, and, vice-versa, knowing the loving God brings anguish and terror to an end.

It is the God of Jesus, then, who is "the secret of the kingdom of God," the God he calls Abba, "my Father and your Father," as he says in John, "my God and your God." Or if we speak of "the secrets of the kingdom" in the plural, they are the ways of his God described in his parables. To know his God I have to enter into his relationship with God. "No one knows the Son except the Father," he says in Matthew, "and no one knows the Father except the Son and anyone to whom the Son chooses to reveal him."[15] It is the relationship, the "I and thou," that defines what is meant by "the loving God." It is the relationship that is implicit in the Lord's Prayer. I enter into relation with his God by dwelling in the particulars of the name, the kingdom, the will, the bread, the forgiveness, the guiding and guarding from temptation and evil. Although this all seems very simple, it is very different from the common notion of God where, instead of praying for the will of God to be done on earth as it is in heaven, everything that happens on earth is the will of God.

If we keep to Mark, we do not have the Lord's Prayer but we do have all its elements, the name (Abba), the kingdom ("the kingdom of God is at hand"), the will ("not what I will, but what thou wilt"), the bread ("Give ye them to eat" and "Take, eat"), the forgiveness ("My son, your sins are forgiven"), the guiding and guarding from temptation and evil ("Watch and pray that you may not enter into temptation"). Is this "the God of Small Things"? You might conclude that from Matthew and Luke where Jesus speaks of sparrows. I remember as a child linking God in my imagination with sparrows. Jesus says there "not one of them will fall to the ground without your Father's will," "not one of them is forgotten before God."[16] Here is where he is closest to the common notion of God. But his point is the loving God, "Fear not, you are of more value than many sparrows."[17]

"The God of Loss? The God of Small Things?"[18] The parables point us beyond loss, beyond small things. "Instead, seek his kingdom, and these things shall be yours as well."[19] Here is where Kafka's parable of parables seems to hold true, "If you only followed the parables you yourselves would become parables and with that rid of all your daily cares." But if the exchange that follows also holds true ("I bet that is also a parable. You have won. But unfortunately only in parable. No, in reality: in parable you have lost"), then in reality our lives are defined by our daily cares and by small things and by loss. It is *when we realize the story we are living in is a story,* when we realize the God of Loss, the God of Small Things belongs to our story, it is then that a reality greater than ourselves begins to shine through, and our lives become "a changing image of eternity," a parable of this greater reality, a mystery. What I mean here is "the mystery of the kingdom of God" in Mark, "the mysteries of the kingdom of heaven" in Matthew, "the mysteries of the kingdom of God" in Luke, using now the King James Version, "mystery" and "mysteries" instead of the Revised Standard Version, "secret" and "secrets." The Greek words here are *mysterion* and *mysteria.* I take mystery to be, like time, "a changing image of eternity" where eternity "shows itself and at the same time withdraws."

Time is the mystery, or rather eternity showing itself and withdrawing in time. "The time is fulfilled, and the kingdom of God is at hand," Jesus begins his teaching in Mark, "repent, and believe in the gospel."[20] Our daily cares, loss, small things all belong to time, but to say "the time is fulfilled, and the kingdom of God is at hand" is to say time is at an end and eternity is breaking through, that our daily cares and loss and small things are at an end, and yet if eternity "shows itself and at the same time withdraws," they are and are not at an end. They are at an end only insofar as we follow the parables and become ourselves parables and heart-free toward our cares, only in our relation to them. That is what it means to "repent, and believe in the gospel," it seems, to come into a new relation with our daily cares, with loss, with the things of life.

Is this foreign to the Gospel, the thought of a mystery that "shows itself and at the same time withdraws"? No, I think this is the very thought that is being conveyed by teaching in parables. It is the hide-and-seek of mystery, showing itself and at the same time withdrawing, that comes through in parables. I take it then "the kingdom of God is at hand" does not mean the literal end of the world as in the "eschatology" of classical biblical criticism. It means the mystery is showing itself in the teaching and miracles of Jesus, but the mystery is also and at the same time withdrawing. Thus the Gospel of Mark has been called the Gospel of "secret epiphanies,"[21] for again and again Jesus will work a miracle and show himself but then enjoin secrecy and withdraw. The transfiguration story, told in Matthew and Mark and Luke, is a story of showing and then withdrawing.[22] In John the showing is in the coming of Jesus and the withdrawing is in his going, his return to the Father.

Why this hide-and-seek, this showing and withdrawing? It is perhaps the nature of a human relation with God, a relation in time with the Eternal. It is certainly true to life, something we experience also in the ebb and flow of human relations. Here the flow is in the showing, the ebb is in the withdrawal. "If he held her, he couldn't kiss her. If he kissed her, he couldn't see her. If he saw her, he couldn't feel her," Arundhati Roy says, describing a dream in her novel *The God of Small Things*. "Who was he, the one-armed man? Who *could* he have been? The God of Loss? The God of Small Things?"[23] There is something tantalizing about the mystery that "shows itself and at the same time withdraws." To relate to God I have to relate to this showing and withdrawing.

Loss is linked with withdrawal. When you go through loss, for instance the loss of a friend, God seems to withdraw, seems to be "The God of Loss." Small things, on the other hand, are linked with showing, with "the mystery of encounter," for instance when you unexpectedly encounter a friend, when you "find friends on your way when you least look for it,"[24] and God seems to show himself, to be "The God of Small Things." The Parable of the Mustard Seed is about the small and the great, how the great becomes the small, the kingdom becomes a seed, and how the small becomes the great, the seed becomes a kingdom.[25] In that way God is indeed "The God of Small Things." Is God then also "The God of Loss"? That may in fact be "the secret of the kingdom of God" or "the mystery of the kingdom of God" as Mark understands it, the secret or mystery of the cross, as in the saying "If anyone would come after me, let him deny himself and take up his cross and follow me. For whoever would save his life will lose it; and whoever loses his life for my sake and the gospel's will save it."[26]

It is clear, though, that loss here is not simply loss, and small things are not simply small things. There is loss, and there are small things in every life, but if loss is not simply loss and small things are not simply small things, there is a mystery at work in every life, a mystery of losing and finding, of the great becoming small and the small becoming great. I can see the losing but where is the finding? I can see the small but where is the great? Here again the answer may be in "the simplicity of vision," the vision of my life as a journey with God in time. What is loss and what is gain, what is great and what is small looks very different in the perspective of the journey. *Solvitur ambulando.* "It is solved by walking."[27] It is solved, really, not just by walking but by walking with God.

If I walk with the God of Jesus, however, I walk with a God for whom "all things are possible," for whom "both-and" is possible, not just "either-or." So the God of Jesus then is not a "one-armed man," and in that sense is not the God of Loss, the God of Small Things. It is true, in my own choices there is an "either-or," if I take one road I will not have taken another, and so there is always in my life a "road not taken," always someone or something I have had to give up in order to take the road I have taken. But God is abundant, the God of Jesus is abundant. After Jesus says "all things are possible with God," Peter says "Lo, we have left everything and followed you" and Jesus replies in the Gospel of Mark, "Truly, I say to you, there is no one who has left house or brothers or sisters or mother or father or children or lands, for my sake and for the gospel, who will not receive a hundredfold now in this time, houses and brothers and sisters and mothers and children and lands, with persecutions, and in the age to come eternal life."[28] To me, always haunted by "the road not taken," this speaks strongly but mysteriously, and says what I have given up I will find again somehow, even in this life.

"Either-or" then holds true of our choices, and "the one-armed man" presides, the God of Loss, the God of Small Things, and there is always "the road not taken." And so we are always tempted to cross the boundaries created by our choices, like the characters in Roy's novel, *The God of Small Things.* "They all crossed into forbidden territory," she says. "They all tampered with the laws that lay down who should be loved and how. And how much."[29] "Both-and" holds not so much for "What should I do?" as for "What may I hope?" It is as in the Parable of the Seed Growing Secretly, a parable that appears only in the Gospel of Mark.[30] I plant the seed, and the seed grows secretly I know not how, and in the harvest I find not only all I have chosen but all I have lost, and I find it a hundredfold.

If I follow Christ, therefore, I encounter the "either-or" in having to leave everyone and everything else behind, but then I encounter the "both-and" in receiving everyone and everything back a hundredfold. As I see it, what this amounts to is simply walking with God, walking with the God of Jesus, walking with a God who is abundant and who is not outdone in generosity. The paradigm here is the story of Solomon's dream where God says "Ask what I shall give you" and Solomon answers "an understanding mind"[31] and God, very pleased with this request, gives him not only all he asked but also all he did not ask. To follow Christ, I gather, is to have "an understanding mind" or to desire it or to choose it, to choose wisdom, a mind for understanding "the secrets of the kingdom," and to share the understanding with others, to sow the seed of understanding. This then is to walk with the God of Jesus, to be a sower who goes out to sow, as in the parable. And here too is the mystery of the cross, if we extend the parable by means of the psalm, "They that sow in tears shall reap in joy."[32]

Is it possible then simply *to choose wisdom?* Is it possible to act as if God were saying to me too "Ask what I shall give you?" To me it does seem possible, for what it means is to follow "the simplicity of vision." I think of a saying I found in Tolkien's last story, *The time has come. Let him choose.*[33] When I have come to "the simplicity of vision" in my life, the time has come for me to choose. It is as if "The time is fulfilled, and the kingdom of God is at hand" for me. My choice then is to follow "the simplicity of vision" and to share the vision with others. "Listen! A sower went out to sow. . . ." But what is the vision? It is simply that of walking with God. For me it is that of my life as a journey in time and God as my companion on the way.

There is an "either-or" in choosing wisdom, a choice between wisdom and foolishness, especially in later life as in the saying "No fool like an old fool," and there is a "both-and" in obtaining wisdom, not both wisdom and foolishness but as in the saying "All good things came to me along with her."[34] Reading the Gospel of Mark for wisdom, I find the "either-or" in the passages on following Christ, leaving everyone and everything else behind, and I find the "both-and" in the promises of Christ, the hundredfold. If the "either-or" answers the question "What should I do?" and the "both-and" answers the question "What may I hope?" what answers the prime question "What can I know?" I suppose it is "the secret of the kingdom of God" or "the mystery of the kingdom of God," and that, according to what we have been saying, is Abba, the God of Jesus. My journey with God in time is an "I and thou" where I enter the solitude of Jesus with Abba. A great stillness comes upon me, if I may paraphrase Tolkien,[35] and I seem to be both in this world and the other, and also outside them and surveying them, so that I am at once in bereavement and in ownership and in peace.

There is bereavement in leaving all else to follow a path, and there is ownership in the hope of all good things coming to me along with wisdom, and there is peace, "his will is our peace," in the sense of following somehow a divine call. I can feel all three of these things: sometimes the sense of bereavement is uppermost, sometimes the sense of hope, and sometimes the sense of peace. But the bereavement and the hope seem to be overtones. The fundamental tone seems to be the peace, the stillness, a great stillness such as you feel when you walk among the giant redwood trees. Maybe then this really is wisdom for me!

The Parables of Knowledge

"Seek peace, and ensue it."[36] That has to be my motto as I seek the wisdom of the parables, as I seek to enter the solitude of Jesus with Abba, as I seek that stillness where I am both in this world and in the other, where I am at once in having and not having and in peace. There is in coming to peace a process of "getting rid of what you haven't got,"[37] specifically of getting rid of what is owed to you by others, getting rid of it by remitting their debts. That is a theme of the Lord's Prayer and also of a parable that occurs only in the Gospel of Matthew, the Parable of the Unmerciful Servant.[38] When I release others, I am released myself, and vice-versa when I do not release them, I am not released myself. What is more, when I do release I come to know God, the loving and forgiving God, and when I am released I come to know myself in having and not having and in peace. Knowing comes of releasing, therefore, of releasing and being released, and the knowing is of God and of myself, as in Saint Augustine's prayer in soliloquy, *noverim me, noverim te,* "May I know me. May I know thee."[39]

"May I know me." Getting rid of the love I haven't got, I come to discover the love I have, and that is knowing me, knowing my love. But what is my love? "Our heart is restless until it rests in you." That is Augustine's answer. That is my answer too, but there is something I learn, entering into the Lord's Prayer, dwelling in its particulars, the name, the kingdom, the will, the bread, the forgiveness, the guiding and the guarding. The forgiveness is my way in, getting rid of what I haven't got, getting rid of what I expect from others, of what I think they owe me, releasing them and being released into "the simplicity of vision" I find in the "I and thou," in the solitude of Jesus with Abba. If I make his "thou" my "thou," then his "I" becomes my "I," I find myself in him. You discover who you are when you discover who Christ is, Matthew seems to say, coupling "You are the Christ . . . ," Peter's affirmation of Christ, with "You are Peter . . . ,"[40] Christ's affirmation of Peter, and you discover who Christ is when you enter into the solitude of Jesus with Abba.

"May I know thee." Getting rid of the love I haven't got, I find the love I have, the love of the same but now in the form of forgiveness, of releasing and being released. Here I am using simultaneously two rather different ways to God, the negative way of

letting go and the affirmative way of finding God in human relations. I am following the negative way in getting rid of the love I
haven't got, but I am following the affirmative way in letting the
love I have be a way into the "I and thou" of Jesus with God.
Interpreting the "I and thou" in terms of the Lord's Prayer, I see
myself standing in his relation with God, entering into his solitude with Abba. I let the Lord's Prayer speak to me as I say the
words to God, letting it reveal God to me and reveal me to me.
The impossible becomes possible in prayer, as Origen says in his
commentary on the Lord's Prayer,[41] the impossible love, I want to
say, becomes possible.

How does an impossible love become possible? Separation is
overcome in prayer, I believe, by union with God, for being in
touch with God I am in touch with everyone I love. It is in the
parable of a camel going through the eye of a needle that this idea
occurs of the impossible becoming possible. "With men this is
impossible, but with God all things are possible," Jesus says in
Matthew; "With men it is impossible, but not with God, for all
things are possible with God," he says in Mark; and "What is impossible with men is possible with God," he says in Luke.[42] What
would it be to see all things through the eye of a needle?

"God is that all things are possible," Kierkegaard says, thinking
of these passages, "and that all things are possible *is* God."[43] There
is a knowledge of God here, a knowledge that arises out of faith in
God, faith in the God of Jesus. The parable of the camel passing
through the eye of a needle is about a rich man being saved with
difficulty, like the rich young man who was unwilling to leave
all and follow Jesus. "Again I tell you, it is easier for a camel to
go through the eye of a needle than for a rich man to enter the
kingdom of God," he says to the astonishment of his disciples.
"Who then can be saved?" they ask. And then he says "with God
all things are possible." So it seems he is saying all can be saved,
rich and poor alike, insofar as all is possible for God. I see in this
a maxim like *distinguer pour unir,* "to distinguish in order to
unite," to distinguish rich and poor in order to unite them all in a

universal salvation. So the knowledge of God here is a knowledge that seems to move toward something like a universal reconciliation of all human beings. All the more does it move toward the possibility of an impossible love.

Getting rid of what I haven't got, of the love I wanted and haven't got, I find the love I have, I find it is the love of God, and I find all love in God's love. Or so it seems when I touch the love of God and feel joy at the thought of my life as a journey with God in time. All the same I am haunted by the love I wanted and haven't got. It is said that the central insight in the teaching of Jesus is the power of forgiveness.[44] That is the miracle working power in Christianity. It is the power to release others from the past and thus to be released oneself from the past and to become open to the future that he calls "the kingdom of God" or "the kingdom of heaven." Haunted as I am by the love I wanted and haven't got, I hope for the miracle. But if his teaching is true, I have already the power to release and be released, the power has been given to me. I have only to believe in it, and to take my freedom as a gift.

So then "To distinguish in order to unite," *distinguer pour unir*, can be a key to the parables that occur only in the Gospel of Matthew and are about distinguishing the wheat and the weeds in a field, the good and the bad in a catch of fish, the obedient and the disobedient son, the wedding guests who have and do not have a wedding garment, the wise and the foolish virgins, and the sheep and the goats. The distinguishing is clear but where is the uniting? There is a uniting in the beginning ("Let both grow together until the harvest") but a separating in the end ("and at harvest time I will tell the reapers . . .").[45] Is there a hint of a further step, a reunion after separation? There may be such a hint in the Sermon on the Mount, "be perfect as your heavenly Father is perfect," when Jesus is speaking of love of enemies "so that you may be sons of your Father who is in heaven; for he makes his sun rise on the evil and on the good, and sends rain on the just and on the unjust."[46]

Perfect love is a sun that rises on the evil and the good, a rain that falls on the just and on the unjust. It is able to distinguish but it is also able to unite. An impossible love, an unrequited love, becomes possible in forgiveness, in releasing and being released from the inner exigencies of love. And so there is a kind of detachment in perfect love. And there is a knowledge of God too in "be perfect as your heavenly Father is perfect," a knowledge that moves me beyond "The God of Loss," beyond "The God of Small Things," especially when I am troubled by loss, troubled by small things. As G. W. Stonier says, "so many clowns have been small . . . pathetic; here is one large and heart-whole."[47] I may be heart-broken with loss, but instead of being unforgiving and becoming small and pathetic I can be forgiving and become "large and heart-whole." If I become bitter, I do indeed become "small . . . pathetic," but if I can forgive, if I can release others and be released myself, I find healing and wholeness of heart. What is more, I come to the sense of a forgiving God.

There is a knowing then that comes of letting go of love, letting go of the love I wanted and don't have, but that letting go is itself a greater love, the love of God. That discovery is the theme of two parables that occur only in the Gospel of Matthew, the Parable of the Treasure and the Parable of the Pearl.[48] Actually the treasure and the pearl are "the kingdom of heaven," and indeed when I realize the love I have is the love of God, that for me is the kingdom. Discovering the love of God, I pass from "human bondage" to "human freedom," as Spinoza says, in "the power of understanding."[49] "Getting rid of what you haven't got" in these parables takes the form of selling all you have in order to buy the pearl or to buy the field in which you discovered the treasure. That sounds more like getting rid of what you have than getting rid of what you haven't got. If we put it in terms of love, however, what you *have* corresponds to the love you haven't got, as in the saying from Proverbs, "Better is a dinner of herbs where love is than a fatted ox and hatred with it," or vice-versa, as George Colman says, "Love and a cottage! Eh, Fanny! Ah, give me indifference and a coach and six!"[50] The fatted ox or the coach and six are what you have corresponding to the love you haven't got.

Is it "the power of understanding," though, that carries us from "human bondage," troubled by loss and by small things, to "human freedom," realizing the love of God? It is if we take it to be also the power of forgiveness. It is the love I wanted and haven't got that stands in my way, that prevents me from understanding the love I have. Releasing others, then, from my expectations, I am released into understanding the love there is in my life. We love with a love we do not know, I have come to believe, and so the essential thing is coming to know the love we do not know, coming to know the love of God. In Matthew and Mark this is one of the "subtle questions" that are posed to Jesus toward the end of his public life, the tribute money, the resurrection, and the great commandment.

Love is the great commandment, according to his answer, to love God "with all your heart, and with all your soul, and with all your might," as is said in Deuteronomy, "and with all your mind," as is added in the Gospels, and to love your neighbor "as yourself."[51] What is it to love "with all your mind"? Here again I think of Malebranche's saying, "Attention is the natural prayer of the soul." Loving with all your mind is watching and praying. The command "Watch!" occurs in Matthew and Mark and Luke,[52] and it is linked with the Parable of the Fig Tree, that of the Master's Return, and that of the Wise and Foolish Virgins. All of these are parables of waiting on God, watching and waiting, watching and praying. It would be easy to pass them off as having to do with an imminent world's end that never came, but it is possible instead to let them speak to the heart like the last of Rilke's *Stories of God*, where a man and a woman are waiting together on the God who "was" and who "will be."[53] If I have learned to wait on God, "I have learned to look close at most things that come my way," like Merlin, knowing I know the God who "was" and don't yet know the God who "will be" but confident the One who "was" and "will be" is one and the same.

"We are too late for the gods and too early for Being,"[54] Heidegger's saying, implies the contrary, that the God who "was" and the God who "will be" are not one and the same. All the same, his notion of time here is perhaps more pertinent than that of Schweitzer, for whom Jesus "lays hold of the wheel of the world to set it moving on that last revolution which is to bring all ordinary history to a close." When Jesus says "Watch!" in his parables or when he says "Watch and pray!" in the Garden of Gethsemane, he is waiting on God. When I wait on God, I am waiting on the eternal in time, I am waiting on "the singing timelessness of the heart." "Song," as Aquinas says, "is the leap of mind in the eternal breaking out into sound."[55]

"Watch and pray!" When he says that in the Garden of Gethsemane, he is facing a time of insult when, like Virgil in Broch's story, he is "stripped of his name, stripped of his soul, stripped of his least song, stripped of the singing timelessness of his heart."[56] Just before this, though, he sings a hymn with his disciples, "And when they had sung a hymn, they went out to the Mount of Olives."[57] I think of an earlier passage which is a song and at the same time a parable,

> We piped to you,
> and you did not dance;
> we wailed,
> and you did not mourn.[58]

It is a parable of rejection like the later Parable of the Wicked Husbandmen. The hymn then is the reverse, a parable of the kingdom, coming as it does after his saying "I shall not drink again of this fruit of the vine until that day when I drink it new with you in my Father's kingdom."[59] The hymn follows then and is, as David Daube says, the second part of the Hallel, psalms of praise, the shortest of which is the shortest of all the psalms,

> Alleluia, all nations!
> Praise him, all you peoples!
> For great is his steadfast love,
> And his faithfulness is forever, Alleluia![60]

I want to take the song itself as one of faith in the face of death and darkness, a parable of faith in the faithfulness of God in the face of human rejection and abandonment.

There is a Gnostic *Hymn of Jesus* that purports to be this hymn and even contains the lines about piping and dancing and wailing and mourning but turns them around into an invitation to dance.[61] If I set this idea to music myself, I would use simply the lines from Matthew and Luke about piping and dancing and wailing and mourning and enclose them with the essence of the Hallel, which is the one word *alleluia,* and thinking of the "children sitting in the marketplace" that Jesus describes as calling out these lines to one another, I would set the words to the music of the Easter chant "O Filii et Filiae":

> Alleluia, alleluia, alleluia!
> We piped to you, and you did not dance.
> We piped to you, and you did not dance.
> We wailed, and you did not mourn. Alleluia!

There are "echoes from the Gnosis" here, as G. R. S. Mead subtitles his translation of *The Hymn of Jesus,* but in these lines I have set down I think there is a glimpse of the faith of Jesus in the faithfulness of God in the face of human rejection, the contrast between "Alleluia" and "We piped to you, and you did not dance...." There is a movement in the Gospels from faithfulness to faith, from faithful observance especially of the great commandment of love to faith in Jesus, but his own faith is in the faithfulness of God, and if we enter into his solitude with Abba, we come to share in that faith in his God, "for great is his steadfast love, and his faithfulness is forever." That is the motive of *alleluia* here. So there is a gnosis, a knowing of God here, but it is a knowing of God that arises out of faith in God's faithfulness. It is a knowing of faithfulness and steadfast love. It comes of faith, not simply of experience, because it is *in the face of* human rejection and abandonment. If I experience loneliness in my own life, I find God in being "alone with the Alone," but that means not just knowing but being known, "Lord, all my longing is known to thee,"[62] my longing for human companionship, my longing to be unalone.

It is enough somehow to know all my longing is known to God, even if my longing is not fulfilled. I think of a passage in Kafka's diary where he speaks of his loneliness. "There is no one here who has an understanding for me in full," he writes. "To have even one who had this understanding, for instance a woman, would be to have support from every side. It would be to have God."[63] When I enter into the solitude of Jesus with Abba, I find that understanding, I find that support from every side. I find it, I say, but I find it by believing. I don't mean to say I experience only my own faith. I do feel the support, I do find the understanding, but I find it only insofar as I lean on the support, rely on the understanding. What I have, as in the traditional formula, is "faith seeking understanding," or not just that, I should say, but "faith finding understanding."

What is more, the understanding I find is first of all a being known and only then a knowing. I find "an understanding for me in full," I find "support from every side," I find it by leaning, by relying, by believing. "No one knows the Son except the Father," Jesus says in Matthew, "and no one knows the Father except the Son and anyone to whom the Son chooses to reveal him," as if to say knowing comes of being known, knowing the Father comes of being known as the Son, and being known comes of entering into the relation of the Son with the Father and praying "Our Father who art in heaven. . . ." This experience of being known leads to a knowing, a "vision of God,"[64] as Cusanus says, and this vision, knowing from being known, seems to be the vision out of which Jesus is speaking in the Sermon on the Mount and the parables. So when Peter says "You are the Christ the Son of the living God," Jesus says in Matthew "Blessed are you, Simon Bar-Jona! For flesh and blood has not revealed this to you, but my Father who is in heaven," for again in Matthew "No one knows the Son except the Father." Peter, entering into the relation of Jesus with Abba, has come to understand and to be understood. Simon becomes Peter here, as later Saul becomes Paul.

Still, it is not a full knowing that one comes to from being known. For it is immediately after this that Peter chides Jesus for speaking of suffering and death and is rebuked, "for thou savourest not the things that be of God, but those that be of men."[65] So it is for me, although I know "all my longing is known to thee," I can still feel all my longing and my longing is capable of distorting my vision, so that I savor human rather than divine things. Specifically, the thing that troubles me is, as a friend of mine used to say observing the lives of her friends in later years, "everything is taken away." The sense of being understood by God led her and me to a very different expectation. I suppose this expectation of ours is just what it means to savor human rather than divine things. To go from being understood to understanding is evidently a leap of mind, like song, "the leap of mind in the eternal breaking out into sound."

What would it be to savor divine rather than human things? All the parables are about this, but two that occur only in Matthew speak to it especially, that of the Laborers in the Vineyard and that of the Talents,[66] the one seeming to ignore our differences (all the laborers get the same wage), the other to make too much of our differences (one servant gets five talents, one gets two, one gets only one). "Every one of us is something that the other is not, and therefore knows something—it may be without knowing that he knows it—which no one else knows," George MacDonald says, "and . . . it is every one's business, as one of the kingdom of light and inheritor in it all, to give his portion to the rest."[67] This certainly makes sense of the receiving and the giving, how we are all different and all the same. But what about my friend's lament that in the end "everything is taken away"? That is the very thing that happened to Jesus himself. I think of the Parable of the Narrow Gate in Matthew and Luke.[68] You can pass through the narrow gate, but you can't take anything with you. No person is excluded, but you have to let go of everyone and everything to pass through the portal of death to life.

So in John it is Jesus himself who is the gate. I remember some years ago being at the Ayasofya in Istanbul and seeing the Greek inscription over the door from the Gospel of John,

The Lord said,	if any one
I am	enters,
the door of the	he will be saved,
sheep;	and will go in and out
by me	and find pasture.[69]

There is a connection I can see here between wisdom and letting go of everyone and everything as in death. It is in letting go and being naked with God that I find the answer to the prayer "May I know me. May I know thee." This letting go and being naked with God is passing through the narrow gate, passing through the eye of a needle. This wisdom is seeing through the eye of a needle.

The Parables of Love

Getting rid of the love I wanted and haven't got, I find the love I have, the love of God, and I find myself on "the road of the union of love with God." Dag Hammarskjöld in his diary tells himself "Do not seek death. Death will find you. But seek the road which makes death a fulfillment."[70] I could say to myself in like manner "Do not seek love. Love will find you. But seek the road of the union of love with God." Not seeking love, I gather, is getting rid of the love I wanted and haven't got. Love finding me, on the other hand, is my finding the love I have, the love of God, my joy at the thought of walking with God, of being on a journey in time with God as my companion on the way. The road which makes love a fulfillment, which makes death itself a fulfillment, is "the road of the union of love with God." This is "the narrow way of eternal life whereof Our Saviour speaks in the Gospel," Saint John of the Cross says in his *Dark Night of the Soul,* "along which way the soul ordinarily passes to reach this high and happy union with God."[71]

It is the parables of love in the Gospel of Luke that are best known as parables, that of the Good Samaritan especially and that of the Prodigal Son. There is something about knowledge too, though, in Luke, particularly the idea of knowing what you are doing. There are the words of Jesus on the cross, "Father, forgive them; for they know not what they do."[72] And there is the strange passage in one codex of Luke where Jesus sees a man working on the sabbath and says "Man, if you know what you are doing you are blessed, but if you know not you are cursed and a transgressor of the Law."[73] Love, I want to say, and especially the love of God, is linked with knowing what you are doing.

We love with a love we do not know, I believe, and so it is essential for us to come to know the love we do not know, the love of God. "Our hearts are restless until they rest in you," and so knowing our love comes with resting in God. The sabbath is God's rest and our rest in God, and so that strange saying of Jesus to the man working on the sabbath, "if you know what you are doing you are blessed," seems to imply some spiritual meaning of the sabbath beyond the literal rest. There are two parables that occur only in Luke that have to do with the divine rest, that of the Friend at Midnight and that of the Unjust Judge.[74] There is an African saying, among the Kikuyu people, *Ngai ndagiagiagwo,* "God is not to be pestered,"[75] but these two parables of Jesus are to the opposite intent, God may indeed be pestered and should be pestered, as one friend pesters another at midnight, as the widow pesters the unjust judge. It seems God's rest is not disturbed by our pestering, or if it is disturbed, it seems God wants to be disturbed by our persistent prayer.

"Wisdom is repose in light,"[76] Joubert says, and repose in light, I suppose, is not the same as ordinary rest or repose. I imagine "if you know what you are doing you are blessed" means something like wisdom and repose in light. Not to know what you are doing, on the other hand, is the opposite of wisdom, and those who "know not what they do," according to Luke, are in need of forgiveness. But there is a way through divine forgiveness to wisdom and repose in light, described in a series of parables, the Sinful Woman (or the Two Debtors), the Lost Sheep, the Lost Coin, the Prodigal Son, and the Pharisee and the Publican.[77] There is a great circle in these stories, especially in the Parable of the Prodigal Son, like that in the saying "The love is from God and of God and towards God."

There is something essential in the story of the Prodigal Son: at first he is at home with his father; then he takes leave of his father and goes "into a far country" where he wastes his substance and is reduced to poverty, and then he comes to his senses and returns home where his father receives him with feasting and rejoicing.

Saint Augustine saw his own story in this and that of all creation: "the story of the soul wandering away from God and then in torment and tears finding its way home through conversion is also the story of the entire created order."[78] That saying, "The love is from God and of God and towards God," as uttered by the old Bedouin to Lawrence of Arabia, has its meaning in the context of Islam, coming from God and returning to God. Said again, as I am saying it, in the context of Christianity, it evokes the coming and going of Christ, as in the Gospel of John, but then again it evokes our own coming from God and going back to God with tears, as in the Gospel of Luke. Perhaps that is the characteristic thing in the Christian story, as told by Saint Luke and Saint Augustine, the return to God is with tears, and yet these tears are met with feasting and rejoicing.

"Even love must pass through loneliness,"[79] Wendell Berry writes of "setting out" on this great circle ("He can no longer be at home, he cannot return, unless he begin the circle that first will carry him away"). There is the loneliness of the son, and there is the loneliness of the father. And this loneliness is my experience and is why I want to see in this a journey with God and not just from God and to God. If God is with us all along the great circle, then indeed the love is not only "from God" and "towards God" but also "of God." There is my loneliness, and there is the loneliness of God. I see the loneliness of the son in his misery and then in his coming to his senses when his longing becomes conscious, and I see the loneliness of the father in his watching and waiting and seeing his son from afar.

"I tell you, her sins, which are many, are forgiven, for she loved much," Jesus tells the Pharisee in the story of the Sinful Woman; "but he who is forgiven little, loves little."[80] It is the same in the story of the Prodigal Son, the son who makes the great circle is forgiven much and loves much, but the other son, who stays at home, is forgiven little and loves little. It is the same also in the story of the Pharisee and the Publican, the one is forgiven little and loves little, but the other is forgiven much and loves much. If we connect love with joy, as Spinoza does, and the love of God with joy at the thought of God, then the moral Jesus draws from the parables of the Lost Sheep and the Lost Coin makes sense, "there will be more joy in heaven over one sinner who repents than over ninety-nine righteous persons who need no repentance" or "there is joy before the angels of God over one sinner who repents," and so also in the story of the Prodigal Son, "It was fitting to make merry and be glad, for this your brother was dead, and is alive; he was lost, and is found."[81] There is joy that is love in the great circle from and of and towards God.

If we speak of the great circle of love and see it in these parables, we are close to saying with Juliana of Norwich,

> Sin is behovely, but
> All shall be well, and
> All manner of thing shall be well.[82]

This is how T. S. Eliot quotes her in *Four Quartets*. The word "behovely" is an old word and means "advantageous, profitable, needful," and here it means "needful." Still, sin is not necessary in these parables in the sense that it is inevitable, for if it were inevitable there would be no "ninety-nine righteous persons who need no repentance," there would be no son who stayed at home. It is needful or behovely to complete the great circle of love.

If you are traveling on the great circle of love, "you will meet many foes, some open, and some disguised," as Tolkien says; "and you may find friends upon your way when you least look for it."[83] That is what happens in the Parable of the Good Samaritan. "A man was going down from Jerusalem to Jericho,"[84] and thus was "setting out" and not yet on his way home. I have been on that road, and it really does go *down* from Jerusalem to Jericho. On the way down, then, he falls in with thieves and is beaten and robbed. A priest and a Levite pass him by, but a Samaritan stops and helps him, a friend where he least looks for it, and the Samaritan too was on his way out from home, for he pays the innkeeper to care for the wounded man and says any further expense he will pay when he returns. So two circles intersect here, that of the wounded traveler and that of the Samaritan, and this, we could say, is "the mystery of encounter." The love of neighbor is in the intersecting of the circles of the love of God, and the mystery of encounter is in finding the unknown friend.

There is this making of friends in the Parable of the Unjust Steward, and there is the failure to do so, like the priest or the Levite passing by, in the Parable of the Rich Man and Lazarus. There is in both of these an image of coming or not coming home to God: "make friends for yourselves by means of unrighteous mammon, so that when it fails they may receive you into the eternal habitations" or else "between us and you a great chasm has been fixed, in order that those who would pass from here to you may not be able, and none may cross from there to us."[85] The homecoming is there too in the Parable of the Great Supper, "A man once gave a great banquet . . . ,"[86] like the feast for the Prodigal Son, but there are those who refuse to come, like the older brother of the Prodigal Son. So the great circle of love is completed only if we are willing to complete it.

The "great chasm" here seems to exclude any idea of universal reconciliation, but I suppose it all comes back to the image of passing through the eye of a needle and the idea that with God all things are possible. The problem in the Parable of the Rich Man and Lazarus is the same as that in the story of the Rich Young Man. I gather that those who hold for a universal reconciliation, like Origen, are going on this, that with God all is possible, that the "great chasm" we cannot cross can nevertheless be crossed by God. What strikes me is something in the passage in Matthew, "When the disciples heard this they were greatly astonished, saying Who then can be saved? *But Jesus looked at them* and said to them, With men this is impossible, but with God all things are possible."[87] I find in those words "But Jesus looked at them" (as if he were surprised at their reaction) a hint as to how his sayings are to be interpreted, not narrowly but in the light of his relation with God.

What then is he saying? *Go over!* If "even love must pass through loneliness," love coming from God must pass through loneliness before returning to God, then we must be now in the passage through loneliness. The road leads through loneliness to "the union of love with God." If the essential message of the parables is *Go over*, as Kafka suggests in his parable of parables, then for us it must be to realize "even love must pass through loneliness." I experience the loneliness, but *Go over* means what I am feeling is really love passing through loneliness. It means realizing love, realizing I love God, and letting that realization carry me over from loneliness to love. I am the Prodigal Son coming to my senses "in a far country," I am invited to the Great Supper, I am the traveler on my way from Jerusalem to Jericho, I am the rich man with Lazarus at my gate. *Go over* means complete the great circle of love.

Go over in the Parable of the Rich Man and Lazarus means go over to Lazarus rather than let the distance between you and him become an impassable chasm. Indeed the love that Jesus proclaims, implicit in his relation with God as Abba, is an unconditional love that welcomes publicans and sinners, and the figure of the publican in these stories is the figure of the rich man redeemed. Yet at the same time Jesus seems to be saying, like the Talmud, "God requires the heart."[88] So the Parable of the Prodigal Son seems to be the most complete of the parables and to describe the entire circle of love, coming from God and returning to God with tears, God requiring the heart and the heart requiring God, and the return to God meeting with unconditional acceptance. I take it there is something in us corresponding to all things possible to God, and it is the heart requiring God. There is our will, not the same as our heart's desire, and that corresponds to what is possible to us, our choices, but then there is the heart that requires God and that goes beyond our choices. "The time has come. Let him choose," as Tolkien says, but then "A great stillness came upon him; and he seemed to be both in the World and in Faery, and also outside them and surveying them, so that he was at once in bereavement, and in ownership, and in peace."[89]

Of this last story of his, Tolkien says it is "an old man's story, filled with the presage of bereavement."[90] If I follow the parables and become myself a parable, I too am "filled with the presage of bereavement," and yet, as I think of it, the bereavement is that of "getting rid of what you haven't got" and it leads to discovering the love I have, the love of God, and it brings me at last to the point where I can answer the divine offer, "Ask what I shall give you," as Solomon did, "an understanding mind," or even as Saint Thomas Aquinas did, "nothing, Lord, but you," and in answering I am "at once in bereavement, and in ownership, and in peace." I really do come to wisdom, to "an understanding mind"; I really do come to walk alone with God, to "nothing, Lord, but you."

It is "the eleventh hour" for me in the language of the parables (that of the Laborers in the Vineyard), and so it is essential for me to abandon false hopes and to let the true hope of my life shine forth, "the road of the union of love with God." When I say it is the eleventh hour, I don't mean to invoke "radical eschatology" and interpret the parables in terms of a false hope of world's end. Rather I mean something more like "the presage of bereavement" that Tolkien speaks of, something like the feeling in the Parable of the Rich Fool, the story of the man who says to himself, "Soul, you have ample goods laid up for many years; take your ease, eat, drink, be merry," and God says to him "Fool! This night your soul is required of you; and the things you have prepared, whose will they be?"[91] The letting go of false hopes is "getting rid of what you haven't got," not of what you have—the Rich Fool doesn't have what he thinks he has. I think of the introduction to *The Spiritual Canticle* by Saint John of the Cross, where he invokes all sorts of biblical images of urgency to lead into his poem about the mystic road of love.

"Where have you hidden, Beloved, and left me with my sadness (*con gemido*)?"[92] he begins, for time here is time in which eternity is hidden and time itself is "filled with the presage of bereavement." I think also of the Parable of the Bridegroom, "The days will come, when the bridegroom is taken away from them, and then they will fast in those days." That is the imagery here. Joy comes with the presence of the Beloved, "Can you make wedding guests fast while the bridegroom is with them?"[93] For me sadness comes of time "filled with the presage of bereavement," and joy comes when "the presage of bereavement" gives way to the sense of going with God on the journey in time.

Time thus is the mystery of the parables, not time empty of eternity but time full of eternity, full of mystery "which shows itself and at the same time withdraws," and following the parables means letting be (Meister Eckhart's *Gelassenheit*) and openness to the mystery. If we read the parables with a sense of time empty of eternity, then "the time is fulfilled, and the kingdom of God is at hand" can only mean the end of time. Thus the "radical eschatology" of which Albert Schweitzer speaks in *The Quest of the Historical Jesus*. If we read them with a sense of time full of eternity, on the other hand, then the kingdom of God "shows itself and at the same time withdraws" in Jesus. I see this changing sense of time (not the interpretation of the parables) in Martin Heidegger's intellectual odyssey, from "time as the possible horizon for any understanding whatsoever of being," as he says at first, to time as "the lighting up of the self-concealing,"[94] as he says later, the lighting up or showing of the mystery that at the same time withdraws or conceals itself.

Parables then are the lighting up of the self-concealing kingdom of God. This notion of time, "the lighting up of the self-concealing" (*die Lichtung des Sichverbergens*), seems to make sense of what Jesus says of parables and of teaching in parables, speaking in Mark of "the secret of the kingdom of God," in Matthew of "the secrets of the kingdom of heaven," in Luke of "the secrets of the kingdom of God." The paradox here is between the showing and the hiding, between "the lighting up" and "the self-concealing." I take those secrets to be the secrets of the love of God, which remain secret, as Ramon Lull says, even after they are revealed, except to those who love. Coming to the parables with my own presage of bereavement, I find hope in them, almost I could say "a secret hope," the hope there is on "the road of the union of love with God."

It is possibility that gives rise to hope, a way where it seemed there was no way, and for me love's road is "the way of possibility."[95] I see here an answer to Saint Augustine's prayer, "May I know me. May I know thee" (*noverim me, noverim te*). For to know God is to know all is possible, as Jesus says of passing through the eye of a needle. What is more, the impossible becomes possible in prayer, as Origen says, and Jesus prays in Mark's account of the Garden of Gethsemane, "Abba, Father, all things are possible to thee . . . ," and Mary hears the angel say in Luke's account of the Annunciation, ". . . For with God nothing will be impossible."[96] There is a story by Isak Dinesen, also a wonderful little Danish film, "Babette's Feast," like the story of the Great Supper or even that of the Last Supper, where the impossible becomes possible, where an impossible love between a man and a woman becomes possible, because they are living in each other's hearts, for "grace is infinite."

"We tremble before making our choice in life, and after having made it again tremble in fear of having chosen wrong," it is said in "Babette's Feast." "But the moment comes when our eyes are opened, and we see and realize that grace is infinite."[97] That moment comes for me in realizing all our loves are one love, in seeing the great circle of love, in knowing "the love is from God and of God and towards God." Our choices have to do with what is possible to us, but infinite grace has to do with our heart's desire and what is possible to God, and so on the great circle of love we find not only our choice in life but also our heart's desire.

Paradoxes

His will is our peace
(la sua volontate è nostra pace)
—*Paradiso* 3:85

To say "grace is infinite" is to say, as in the Gospel of John, "God does not give the Spirit by measure."[1] What then may I hope? There is a combination of willingness and hope in faith, a willingness to die and yet a hope to live, a willingness to walk alone and yet a hope of companionship on the way, a willingness to leave all and follow Christ and yet a hope to receive all back a hundredfold. It is not so much a limit on hope as a balance between hope and willingness. This balance appears in the paradoxes of the teaching of Jesus, especially in the Beatitudes, as if he were saying, "Blessed are those who are willing, for hope belongs to them."

There is a saying in the Garden of Gethsemane, according to Matthew and Mark, that may be a key to the Beatitudes, "the spirit indeed is willing, but the flesh is weak."[2] Also in the Garden there is the combination of willingness and hope, the hope of "Abba, Father, all things are possible to you" and the willingness of "yet not what I will but what thou wilt" in Mark, or in Matthew, "if it be possible" and "not as I will but as thou wilt," or in Luke, "if thou art willing" and "not my will, but thine, be done."[3] The Beatitudes in

Matthew then are those of the willing spirit: the poor in spirit, those who mourn, the meek, those who hunger and thirst for righteousness, the merciful, the pure in heart, the peacemakers, those who are persecuted for righteousness' sake. And the hope is the kingdom, to be comforted, to inherit the earth, to be satisfied, to obtain mercy, to see God, to be called the children of God, to enter the kingdom of heaven.[4] The Beatitudes in Luke are of those who suffer: the poor, the hungry, the weeping, the persecuted.[5] I take it the willingness there is to go through suffering and the hope to come into happiness. The paradox of all these sayings is "happy are the unhappy."

A gnostic turn is given to these paradoxes in *The Gospel according to Thomas,* a turn comparable to that in *The Gospel of Truth,* where gnosis consists essentially of knowing the Father, knowing the loving God. If I am willing to die and yet hope to live, willing to walk alone and yet hope to find companionship on the way, willing to leave all and follow Christ and yet hope to receive all back again a hundredfold, I come to know God as a loving God. But if I start at the other end, knowing the loving God, I can encounter something in my life that is profoundly against my will, and that can make it seem to me the loving God is an illusion, or that what is against my will cannot be from the loving God but must be from some other power.

Say I do come upon something, a loss of someone in my life, that is against my will. If I accept this loss as somehow belonging to the will of God for me, then I take my stand in faith rather than in gnosis, I take my stand in willingness and hope.

"Become passers-by"[6] is the shortest saying in *The Gospel according to Thomas.* It is a way of saying, as in the parables, "Go over." I don't think it means to become passers-by like the priest and the Levite who pass by the wounded man on the road but to become passers-by like the Good Samaritan who turns toward rather than turning away, who is open to the mystery of encounter. To be open to the mystery of encounter, however, I have to take my stand in willingness and hope, taking the chance meetings of life as significant.

Now if we leave aside beatitudes that occur also in the canonical gospels such as "Blessed are the poor . . ." and consider just those that occur only in *The Gospel according to Thomas,* we get a rather strange list:

> Blessed is the lion which the man eats and the lion will become man; and cursed is the man whom the lion eats and the lion will become man.
> Blessed is he who shall stand at the beginning, he shall know the end and he shall not taste death.
> Blessed is he who was before he came into being.
> Blessed are the solitary and elect, for you shall find the kingdom; because you come from it, and you shall go there again.[7]

If I may introduce an African saying, "The Lion is God,"[8] I can make a kind of sense of the first beatitude. The metaphor is that of eating God and being eaten by God so that God becomes man. All four of these beatitudes then seem to be describing the great circle of coming from God and returning to God. What is missing again is the combination of willingness and hope, "Blessed are those who are willing, for hope belongs to them."

If I take my stand in gnosis, I know I come from God and return to God, I know "the love is from God and of God and towards God," but I can pass by the mystery of encounter. If I take my stand in faith, on the other hand, I am more conscious of knowing we love with a love we do not know, if I take my stand in willingness and hope, I turn toward the mystery of encounter, taking the chance meetings of life as significant. "Now they had to trust each other," as Jim Henson says in his story *The Dark Crystal,* "or else the world transformed by their chance meeting, would become a place without meaning or future after all, a place merely of chance."[9]

Trusting God is very close to trusting each other. It is a fundamental attitude toward the encounters and situations of life. I think of "abandonment to divine providence"[10] as Jean-Pierre de Caussade calls it. I think of it in the chance meetings of life. I think of it also in the losses and disappointments of life. "His will is our peace" is my criterion for discerning the will of God in these things. When I find peace in relation to an encounter or a loss or a disappointment in my life, I believe I have found the will of God. I am not so far from gnosis in this, for I am finding the will of God not simply in the things that happen but in my relation to the things, not any relation but the relation that brings inner peace. I am submitting my own will not simply to the things of my life but to the inner light in which I see the things and discern the relation that is the will of God. Submission to the will of God, then, means submission to the inner light, and that is close to gnosis. There is the combination of willingness and hope, nevertheless, in the Yes to the will of God and the peace, willingness in the Yes and hope in the peace.

I am close enough to gnosis to make sense of these strange gnostic beatitudes. If I have found in life not only chance meetings that have issued into mutual trust but also loss and disappointment, I am able to see the great circle of love coming from God and returning to God as the real meaning of my life. "In my beginning is my end," as T. S. Eliot says in *Four Quartets,* and "In my end is my beginning."[11] What then may I hope? If love of God is simply joy at the thought of God, as Spinoza says, I may hope to live in the joy of being on a journey in time with God as my companion on the way.

I have always thought of the Beatitudes, especially as given in Matthew, as a kind of summary of the teaching of Jesus, like the Lord's Prayer, or like the Four Noble Truths as a summary of the teaching of Buddha ("All egocentric life is suffering. This suffering is caused by misknowing and its consequences. There is a real freedom from this suffering. The path to that freedom is eightfold").[12] The Beatitudes too are eightfold, and there is an insight there into suffering. If I meditate on the Beatitudes now in the light of the great circle of love coming from God and returning to God, I see the paradoxes of suffering in a new light. "God requires the heart" and sometimes God requires us to sacrifice what is most dear, like Abraham sacrificing Isaac, and indeed in death we have to let go of everyone and everything. So if God requires my heart in this way, I find peace nevertheless in accepting the will of God, I find indeed "His will is our peace." What the Beatitudes say, I believe, is that if you are willing to sacrifice what is most dear, you are blessed, and your hope will not be disappointed, "Blessed are the poor in spirit, for theirs is the kingdom of heaven. . . ."

In dealing with loss and disappointment the great danger is to fall into bitterness and cynicism. I find myself repeating that prayer, "Keep me friendly to myself, keep me gentle in disappointment." All I know of the will of God in whatever happens to me, if I use the criterion "His will is our peace," is my own relation to it, friendly to myself and gentle in disappointment. That friendliness and gentleness relates especially to the first three of the Beatitudes, "Blessed are the poor in spirit . . . those who mourn . . . the meek. . . ." That friendliness to myself has to do also with my heart's longing, "Blessed are those who hunger and thirst for righteousness" and "Blessed are the pure in heart," and that gentleness has to do with my relation with others, "Blessed are the merciful" and "Blessed are the peacemakers" and "Blessed are those who are persecuted for righteousness' sake." I can see in this last something similar to Socrates saying "I would rather suffer injustice than do it."[13]

If I compare the Beatitudes with the Four Noble Truths, I can see the apparent difference is in the Buddhist doctrine of "no self,"[14] the thought that selfhood is the root of suffering, and freedom from suffering is in letting go of self. In Christianity the ability to love depends on the willingness to go through suffering. Here again there is the combination of willingness and hope. So "the sense of I" is intact in Christianity, though there is "the denial of self" in following Christ. Self-denial is simply the willingness to go through suffering. All the same, the passage from will to willingness is very close to the letting go of self in Buddhism, for the prime meaning of self is will, as when a little child says "No" and "mine," "No" is will and "mine" is self. So the long spiritual journey from "No" and "mine" to "Yes" and "yours" is a journey through will to willingness. The deeper sense of "I" then is in willingness or indeed in willingness and hope and in the peace at our "center of stillness surrounded by silence."

All I know of the will of God, therefore, standing in my center of stillness, is my relation to it, or my relation to what happens in the light of inner peace. "Abandonment to divine providence" is a letting be, a releasement toward what happens, and an openness to the mystery in what happens, but the mystery is still mystery to me. So I take my stand in faith rather than in gnosis, I take my stand in willingness and hope, my willingness in releasement toward the things that happen, my hope in openness to the mystery. My knowing then, instead of knowing I know, is knowing I do not know. It is like "the cloud of unknowing in the which a soul is oned with God."[15] There is a union of wills, my will and God's will, in releasement and openness to the mystery.

"There are also times in life when a person has to rush off in pursuit of hopefulness,"[16] Jean Giono says, making a distinction between hope (*espoir*) where one's heart is set on someone or something and hopefulness (*esperance*) where one's heart is open to the mystery. When my heart has been set for a long time on someone or something and has come to loss or disappointment, then it is time for me to rush off in pursuit of hopefulness. Something like this seems to have happened to the disciples of Jesus at his death. "We had hoped that he was the one to redeem Israel"[17] the two disciples say on the way to Emmaus. When they meet with loss and disappointment in his death, they turn from the hope they had to the new hopefulness of his resurrection. The paradox of his life and death illumines the paradoxes of his teaching: the hope of the Beatitudes is a hopefulness open to the mystery. So too if I go from hope to hopefulness, I open myself to the *unexpected* in my life. Instead of going over and over my loss and disappointment, I open myself once more to the mystery that shows and withdraws in my life.

To "rush off in pursuit of hopefulness" is to set out again upon the adventure of my life. I think of the moment in Tolkien's trilogy when Frodo contemplates setting out on his adventure:

He did not tell Gandalf, but as he was speaking a great desire to follow Bilbo flamed up in his heart—to follow Bilbo, and even perhaps
to find him again. It was so strong that it overcame his fear: he could
almost have run out there and then down the road without his hat,
as Bilbo had done on a similar morning long ago.[18]

Setting out again upon the adventure of my life means setting out
again upon the great circle of love that comes from God and goes
to God. It means setting out once again upon "the road of the
union of love with God." It means following Christ. I say "setting
out again" because I can get diverted from the adventure of my
life by setting my heart on someone or something. To set out
again I have to make the move then from *espoir* to *esperance*,
from a heart set on someone or something to a heart open to the
mystery.

"I am with you," the divine answer in times of choice and also
in times of loss and even in times when the dreadful seems already to have occurred, can easily be spurned, for the divine presence is spiritual and intangible. If I embrace the divine presence,
though, I do set out in earnest on the journey with God in time.
I think of the words of Knowledge to Everyman in the medieval
morality play,

> Everyman,
> I will go with thee
> and be thy guide,
> in thy most need
> to go by thy side.[19]

I want to transform this into a prayer, using the form of the Japa-
nese *haiku,* where there are exactly seventeen syllables:

> O Lord, go with me
> and be my guide,
> in my most need
> be by my side.

I like especially that phrase "in my most need." To follow Christ is
indeed to "rush off in pursuit of hopefulness" and it is "in my

most need" when it is time for me to rush off like this, at times when it seems there is no hope and there is no way.

There is this rushing off then in pursuit of hopefulness, like the first disciples following Christ and like them again, after his death, going everywhere with the hopeful news of his resurrection, but as a settled state *esperance* is "the permanent state or condition of living one's life in hopeful tranquillity"[20] and so connects closely with "His will is our peace." There is a difference between inner peace and an inner silence that is a kind of spiritual numbing. When I mistake the will of God, taking some loss or disappointment or even some dreadful occurrence as God's will, I become silent inside, as if numbed. It is only when I see God's will rather in our relation to events, whether they be desired or feared, glad or sad, only when I see God's will for me in my own relation to the events of my life, letting be and being open to the mystery, that I feel the peace.

What this leads to is a great simplicity, the relation of trust that Jesus had with Abba his God. The peace is in that trust, that complete confidence in God. "But although Christ has complete confidence in his father and even feels at one with him," Jung says in *Answer to Job,* "he cannot help inserting the cautious petition—and warning—into the Lord's Prayer: 'Lead us not into temptation, but deliver us from evil.'"[21] Actually, though, that petition has to do with temptation not as enticement to evil but as what my friend David Daube called "the test of loneliness," as in the story of Hezekiah, "God left him to himself, in order to try him and to know all that was in his heart."[22] Not really for God to know but for us to know. Jesus himself undergoes the test of loneliness, "My God, my God, why have you forsaken me?" The divine answer here, and the answer also to Job, is "I am with you." To trust God is to know "I am with you" even in the face of death and darkness when the presence is behind us instead of in front of us. "I am with you" seems to be the essence of the incarnation, Emmanuel, "God with us."

So the paradoxes of the teaching of Jesus are expressions of that combination of willingness and hope that is faith in God, the willingness to die and yet the hope to live, the willingness to walk

alone and yet the hope of companionship on the way, the willingness to leave all and follow Christ and yet the hope of receiving all
back a hundredfold. And if we relate the paradoxes of his teaching
to the paradoxes of his life and death, we find a passage from will
to willingness, as in his agony in the garden, and a passage from
hope to hopefulness, as in the disciples facing his death and coming
to believe in his resurrection. So the deep mystery of Christianity
is in the passage through death to life.

"Faith in God" (*Fe em Deus*) is a sign I saw once over a hut
when I was on a riverboat voyage up the Amazon.[23] The faith that
Jesus speaks of when healing, "Your faith has made you whole,"
and his own faith in Abba his God, is an utter confidence in God.
Infinite resignation is our recognition and acceptance of God's
love, according to Kierkegaard,[24] but faith is our finite repetition
of God's love for us. So it is not completely passive, as you might
be tempted to conclude from the sign over the hut on the
Amazon, but is active enough to heal and be healed. The passive
element in it is that of willingness, the letting be; the active element is that of hope, or more accurately of hopefulness, the openness to the mystery that is able to heal and be healed, to make
whole and become whole. But the wholeness is ultimately not just
health but love, loving "with all your heart, and with all your soul,
and with all your might."

"Unless you hope you will not find the unhoped-for,"[25] Heraclitus' saying, calls for hope to open into hopefulness in order to
embrace the unhoped-for. If my heart is set on someone or something, I will have great difficulty in recognizing the unhoped-for
when it comes. All the same, there is the transcendence of longing, my heart's longing always goes beyond the set of my will. So
it was with the hope of Israel and the coming of Jesus. To recognize in him the hope of Israel was to pass from hope to hopefulness, to pass from will to willingness. So it is too for us now, to recognize in him God-with-us is to embrace the unhoped-for.

As I pass from will to willingness and from hope to hopefulness
in response to Christ, I get a glimpse of his own turning points,
"not as I will but as thou wilt." I am entering into his relation with

Abba, reenacting in my own life the turning points of his life. How far does this go? I find it very difficult to deal with things that are against my own will, living situations for instance that are not my own choice, human relations that do not work out as I wanted and hoped. I have to make the passage from contrary will to willingness in these things in order to find the peace of God's will and also from disappointed hope to hopefulness. I see the deep wisdom of letting be and openness to the mystery. It leads to a greater and deeper life. It is in truth "the road of the union of love with God." Each crisis of will and hope, I see, does bring me into closer touch with God, and I do begin to understand "his commandment is eternal life."

Turning Points

Let not your heart be troubled:
you believe in God, believe also in me.

—John 14:1

I believe in God-with-us. It is true, I see turning points in the life of Jesus, the points where his life crosses that of John the Baptist. As I see them, though, they are points of disclosure where God-with-us is disclosed, in his withdrawal into solitude, in his return to the human circle, in his facing death. They map out for us a way of reading the Gospels. They are his stages on life's way.

"We can know more than we can tell," Polanyi's saying, is especially true of passing over into the life of Jesus and coming back from there to our own lives. If we go with him into the desert, we are entering into his solitude with Abba his God, and we come back into our own solitude with God. If we return with him from the desert to the human circle to proclaim the coming of the kingdom, we are entering into his relation with his disciples and his contemporaries, and we come back from there into the human circle of our own lives. And if we face death with him, we are entering into his willingness and his hope, and we come back from there to face our own death in willingness and hope. We can tell then of solitude, of the human circle, of facing death, but we can know of God-with-us in solitude, in the human circle, and in facing death.

There is a deep loneliness we find in solitude but also in the human circle, a loneliness not taken away by human intimacy, a loneliness we find above all in facing death, and so to find God-with-us in solitude, in the human circle, in facing death, to find God-with-us in that deep loneliness is to know more than we can tell. Yet here I am, telling it. What is meant, though, by "more than we can tell" is telling how. "We know a person's face, and can recognize it among a thousand, indeed among a million," Polanyi says. "Yet we usually cannot tell how we recognize a face we know."[1] There is a kind of recognition in the "I am" sayings in the Gospels. I follow David Daube in taking these as expressions of the Shekinah, the presence of God. They are expressions, I want to say too, of knowing more than we can tell. We recognize God-with-us and yet we are unable to tell, to spell out how we recognize the divine presence just as we are unable to tell how we recognize a face. I suppose the recognition arises out of faith, "you believe in God, believe also in me." I believe in God and so I am able to recognize God-with-us.

Yet there are many who believe in God and who don't recognize God-with-us in Christ. So if we do recognize him, it is because we are dwelling in the particulars of his relation with God by prayer, invoking the name, the kingdom, the will, the bread, the forgiveness, the guiding and the guarding. Let us see what it would be to pass over to Jesus and come back again to ourselves in solitude, in the human circle, and in facing death.

Withdrawing into Solitude

It is by way of prayer that we enter into his solitude with God, praying with him and withdrawing with him into solitude. "Attention is the natural prayer of the soul," Malebranche's saying, does throw light on the prayer of Jesus. If I am waiting on God in solitude, practicing *attente de Dieu,* I have to let be, to let everyone and everything be, everyone and everything in my life, and I have to hold myself open to the mystery that shows itself and at the same time withdraws in my life. My temptation, his temptation in the desert I see, is not to wait, not to let be, not to be open. Waiting on God, letting everyone and everything else be, being open to the mystery, that is what he is doing in the desert. "One who truly remembers my Beloved, in remembering him forgets all things around," Ramon Lull says of remembering Christ; "and one who forgets all things in remembering my Beloved, is defended by him from all harm, and receives a part in all his blessings."[2] For me the remembering is in waiting and openness to the mystery, and the forgetting is in letting go of everyone and everything else.

"I am" has its origin in "I and thou." It is in Mark and Luke that we find the divine voice at his baptism, "You are . . ." (in Matthew it is "This is . . ."), but in John the outer voices of his adversaries seem to echo the inner voices of his temptations, "Are you . . . ?" Somehow out of "You are" and "Are you?" comes "I am." Remembering here for me is to some extent imagining, like Flaubert in his *Temptation of Saint Anthony*.[3] Flaubert does a marvelous job with "Are you . . . ?" but his skepticism keeps him from feeling the force of "You are. . . ." Let us begin then with the beginning of the Gospel of Mark. There are three voices there in the opening chapter, "the voice of one crying in the wilderness," that of John the Baptist, then "a voice from heaven" saying "You are my beloved Son, in whom I am well pleased," and finally the voice of Jesus saying "The time is fulfilled, and the kingdom of God is at hand."

I think again of "the three voices of poetry" as T. S. Eliot calls them, the voice of the One, the voice of the One before the Many, and the voices of the Many. We all have a conversation going on with ourselves, an inner conversation about our hopes and fears, and that is what Eliot means by the first voice, but if we let that conversation with ourselves become a conversation with God, then it becomes what I mean here by the voice of the One, saying "You are my beloved Son. . . ." I see "the voice of one crying in the wilderness" and the voice of Jesus himself announcing the kingdom as the voice of the One before the Many. And I see the many voices of the adversaries of Jesus as well as the inner voices of his temptations as the voices of the Many, though Matthew and Luke treat this third voice as the voice of one, Satan, tempting Christ in the desert. Elsewhere Mark and Luke see this as the voice of the Many, "My name is Legion; for we are many."[4] It is the very nature of this last voice to be manifold, though it is connected in a profound way with the first voice—Eliot speaks of "the octopus or angel with which the poet struggles."[5]

There is something manifold about the octopus with its many tentacles and yet also one with its one head directing all, but by comparison the angel is simply one. All the same, there can be a struggle with the angel as well as the octopus, like Jacob wrestling all night with the angel. Are we to imagine Christ wrestling with God or wrestling with an angel of light as well as wrestling with Satan? The agony in the Garden of Gethsemane is a wrestling with the will of God, sweating blood and ending "not as I will, but as thou." Maybe wrestling belongs to the essence of "I and thou" with God.

"You are my beloved Son, in whom I am well pleased," the "voice from heaven" seems to sum up all his life to this point, an "unconditional relation" with God, as Martin Buber calls it in *I and Thou*. The infancy narratives of Matthew and Luke turn this relation into a story, the story of Jesus the son of Mary. That is what he is called in the Koran, Ibn Maryam, the Son of Mary.[6] To say he is the Son of God, though, as is said in the Gospels, is to speak of the transcendent element in his life. "It may be that a clear sense of the self can only crystallize round something transcendental,"[7] Robert Bolt says in the preface to his play *A Man for All Seasons*. That is what we have here, it seems, in the baptism of Jesus and the voice from heaven, a clear sense of self crystallizing round something transcendental. It is true, Bolt's saying can be true of every life, of our lives as well as the life of Jesus, our own clear sense of self can only crystallize round something transcendental. All the same, there is something unique about the relation of Jesus to the transcendental. Here is how Buber describes it in *I and Thou:*

> And to anticipate by taking an illustration from the realm of unconditional relation: how powerful, even to being overpowering, and how legitimate, even to being self-evident, is the saying of *I* by Jesus! For it is the *I* of unconditional relation in which the man calls his *Thou* Father in such a way that he himself is simply Son, and nothing else but Son.[8]

To be sure, Buber doesn't mean here to affirm the divinity of Christ. He is speaking from a Jewish standpoint, and he goes on to say "every man can say *Thou* and is then *I*, every man can say Father and is then Son: reality abides." Speaking from a standpoint of Christian faith, I want to say that we have here *an eternal I and thou,* not just an eternal thou. But does this not prevent us from passing over into the standpoint of Jesus? No, I want to say, it is still possible to pass over. There are two modes of participation, one is simply by likeness, and that is what Buber has in mind, but the other is by presence, and that is what I have in mind. We are able by passing over to enter, human as we are, into an eternal I and thou. It is thus that we can understand how he, eternal as he is, can be human.

Yet there is something Buber says of God, that God "is not 'immortal' but eternal,"[9] that is very helpful for passing over and seeing how the Eternal can become human and mortal. What Buber is saying is that God is not alien to us like the immortal gods but is near to us, even though God is living and undying. God does not belong to a divine race alien to the human race, but is the creator of human and all other beings. So God is not alien to any of his creations. It is possible, I conclude, to pass over into an eternal I and thou, even though I am mortal. What is more, passing over to God-with-us, I discover the eternal in myself, the eternal in us. I find what Kierkegaard calls "an eternal consciousness" in myself and in all human beings. All the same, I do not thereby discover that I am or we are equivalent to

God-with-us but rather that God-with-us is alive and is present among us.

An eternal consciousness? "If there were no eternal consciousness in a man," Kierkegaard writes in *Fear and Trembling*, "if at the foundation of all there lay only a wildly seething power which writhing with obscure passions produced everything that is great and everything that is insignificant, if a bottomless void never satiated lay hidden beneath all—what then would life be but despair?"[10] Christ calls the unknown Abba, therefore, and not "a wildly seething power" or "a bottomless void." And so if I enter into his solitude with Abba, I learn to call the unknown Abba and to trust in Abba, I call the unknown "thou" as he does and I enter thereby into his relation with God, and because of Abba, because of the eternal thou, I find in myself an eternal I, "an eternal consciousness," and yet not simply an eternal I but something more like the formula in the Gospel of John, "I in them and thou in me," a presence of Christ in me and of Abba in him, for it is his God that is my God, that I set against "a wildly seething power," against "a bottomless void."

"Are you?" therefore, the temptation formulated in Matthew and Luke, "If you are the son of God . . . ," leads back toward "a wildly seething power," toward "a bottomless void," toward "what then would life be but despair?" So do the great questions in John, when they become challenges, "Where do you come from?" and "Where are you going?" Flaubert's structuring of temptation in *The Temptation of Saint Anthony* is very true to life. Saint Anthony experiences first the deprivations of his solitary life, like Christ feeling the hunger in the desert, and then he experiences all sorts of imaginary fulfillment culminating in his imaginary encounter with the Queen of Sheba, and then he imagines encountering his old disciple Hilarion, who fills him with doubts about his life and his beliefs, and then he meets in his imagination all the heretics, one after another, and sees the mixed feelings of the martyrs, and meets the miracle-working Apollonius, who is a kind of false Christ; then he sees the gods, the Buddha, and the twilight of the gods; then the Devil takes him up to see the universe as the work of an impersonal God, and then he sees a phantasmagoria of forms and wants himself to become matter, and at last he sees the face of Christ in the rising sun and returns to his prayers. It is an extravaganza of the imagination.

Of *our* imagination, that is, things that come to mind as we pass over to Christ in the desert. But what of Christ himself? "There is no evidence that Christ ever wondered about himself, or that he ever confronted himself," Jung says in *Answer to Job*. "To this rule there is only one significant exception—the despairing cry from the Cross: 'My God, my God, why hast thou forsaken me?'"[11] It seems to me, on the contrary, that Christ does indeed confront himself in the desert. That is the point of the question "Are you?" implicit in "If you are the son of God. . . ." The temptation is not merely to turn stones into bread or to cast himself recklessly from the pinnacle of the temple but to doubt "You are my beloved Son. . . ." And the answer, his answer, is to trust implicitly in Abba, his God.

There is another temptation in the desert, however, besides the ones that begin "If you are the son of God . . . ," and that is the temptation of an earthly kingdom. There is a reverse of this sequence in Pilate's questions to him in John: first Pilate asks "Are you the King of the Jews?" and Jesus says "My kingdom is not of this world," and then afterwards, hearing him accused of making himself the son of God, Pilate asks "Where are you from?"[12] I take it that the earthly kingdom was a real temptation all his life because of the expectations of his times, and that he set against this his relation with Abba, his God, a spiritual relation, so spiritual that to go with expectations of an earthly kingdom would have been to renounce the worship of God "in spirit and in truth," as it is called in John. Matthew and Luke have him answer the Devil "You shall worship the Lord your God, and him only shall you serve."[13] I gather then that it is his relation with Abba, his God, that is being challenged and clarified in the desert and afterwards in the dialogues with his adversaries. It is this spiritual relation with Abba, his God, that is the core of his life.

If he was the son of God, how can he have been tempted at all? And yet he was the son of God and was tempted. I suppose being tempted goes with being truly human. By relating to myself and willing to be myself, Kierkegaard says, I am "grounded transparently" in God.[14] There can be transparent grounding in my life and yet its transparency depends on relating to myself and willing to be myself, and that is the vulnerable point of attack by temptation, my relating to myself and my willing to be myself. Consider again the prayer, "Keep me friendly to myself, keep me gentle in disappointment." That must be the Achilles' heel, the vulnerable point of every human being, the relation to self and the willingness to be oneself.

"I am," then, is a response to "You are" and "Are you?" but it arises out of "I and thou," out of the relation of Jesus with Abba, his God. I think of the phrase *Retirement for solitary prayer* which occurs again and again, and always in italics, in "The Harmony of the Gospels,"[15] as if the author of the Harmony was very taken with the thought of Jesus retiring into the solitude of prayer. The forty days in the desert were just the first and longest of these episodes. Passing over to Jesus in his retirement for solitary prayer, we enter into his prayer to Abba, his God, praying as he taught his disciples to pray, hallowing the name of his God, praying for God's kingdom to come, for God's will to be done on earth as it is in heaven, for our daily bread (or for the bread from heaven, as Origen says, or today for the bread of the morrow, or for the bread of the Coming One, as David Daube says),[16] for forgiveness as we forgive others, and for guiding and guarding from temptation and evil.

Coming back to ourselves from such prayer, we come back to a sense of divine providence at work in our lives. We come back to lack and loss and letting go, the things that raise questions about divine providence in our lives. It is as if there were something in our lives that has hold of us, like the Ring in Tolkien's trilogy, something we have to let go in order to be heart-free. "It has got far too much hold on you," Bilbo is told. "Let it go! And then you can go yourself, and be free."[17] And when he does let it go he feels relieved and begins to hum the tune "The Road goes ever on and on," and then he sets out on his last adventure. I suppose this is the same as the parable I found in Saint John of the Cross: the bird cannot fly as long as it is tied only by a thread, but once the thread is broken it can fly.

"Love is letting go of fear,"[18] and letting go is perhaps always a letting go of fear, though it can feel more like a letting go of hope. When I let go of a hope of intimacy, I am letting go also of a fear of being alone. Yet there can be a trusting in letting go and so a hope after all. "Love is letting go of fear," a New Age maxim, can hold true apart from the New Age disbelief in evil. It can hold even in the perspective of "Lead us not into temptation, but deliver us from evil," where there is still the fear of evil but love is stronger than fear. Love of God, to be sure, as Spinoza conceives it, joy at the thought of God, while it casts out fear, does not at all involve a trust in divine providence. For Spinoza things simply flow out of God by a kind of inevitability. Einstein had Spinoza's God in mind, it seems, when he said "God does not play dice." If we think of the love of God as a great circle, though, "The love is from God and of God and towards God," then there is a meaning in events, a direction "from and of and towards" that we can discern, not just time's arrow from past to future, but love's direction from God and to God.

At any rate Jesus comes back from his solitude with Abba to say not a sparrow "will fall to the ground without your Father's will." I think of a poem by Jaroslav Seifert where he says "Only a bird knows how to die: falling on to dew-filled grass headfirst."[19] But the saying of Jesus is coming out of a relation of trusting prayer where God is seen as a loving Father who cares even about sparrows and knows them in their living and their dying, and who cares all the more for us who try in dying to rise to the light. "I am," then, is said in the confidence of this love, and it expresses the Shekinah, as David Daube says, the divine presence, as if to say "God is here" or "God is with us." It expresses the "I" of an "I and thou" that is fully expressed in prayer, the "I" of Jesus in his "I and thou" with Abba.

We try in dying to rise to the light instead of "falling on to dew-filled grass headfirst," and Jesus, coming out of the confidence of his relation with Abba, dares to promise us eternal life, and to teach, as Kazantzakis says, "the earth is a path that leads into the sky."[20] That is love's direction, from God and to God, and the way is Jesus' own relation with God, our entering into his intimacy with Abba. All of this depends on prayer, if I am on the right track here, on the prayer of Jesus himself and on our entering into his prayer, and when I say prayer I mean relation with God, an "I and thou," a to-and-fro with God. Everything depends on his relation with God and our entering into his relation and verifying for ourselves what he says. I was present at the meeting on Cape Cod when Erik Erikson presented his approach to all this, "The Galilean Sayings and the Sense of I,"[21] where he said the sayings of Jesus lead us into our own inwardness. I would only add that this inwardness has to become that of prayer in order for us to verify what Jesus is saying, and insofar as everyone has a *thou*, Abba has to become our *thou*.

Who is my *thou*? The prime example of a *thou* in Buber's *I and Thou* is Goethe's *thou*, "God's presence in each element." That is from the epigraph of the book, "So, waiting," Goethe says, "I have won from you the end: God's presence in each element."[22] That corresponds to the Shekinah, the divine presence in the world, but that is what Jesus means by "I am." The *thou* of Jesus is rather the One, the Old One as Einstein calls him, "I want to understand time because I want to get close to the Old One."[23] If I want to get close to the *thou* of Jesus, then I want to get close to the Old One. But how? By understanding time? By "God's presence in each element"? By the "I am" of Jesus? I suppose that is it, I will come through the "I am" of Jesus to his *thou*, Abba.

Still, the sayings of Jesus lead us into our own inwardness, as Erikson says, his "I am" leads me into my own "I am" and so also into "God's presence in each element," as when he walks on the water and says "Take heart, I am (or it is I); have no fear," and into an understanding of the relativity of time, as when he says "before Abraham was, I am."[24] If I meditate on "I am," my own "I am" in the light of his "I am," not to obtain certainty like Descartes so much as to gain understanding, I do "get close to the Old One." Perhaps this is the method rather than that of *A Discourse on Method*, to meditate on "I am" indeed but to meditate on my "I am" in the light of the great "I am" of the Gospels, and to meditate, to understand, rather than to be sure. I find the quest of certainty self-defeating, the more I try to make sure the more unsure I become, but if I go in quest of understanding, I always come to light.

"Light,—more light!" Goethe's last words, show how we try in dying to rise to the light. That rising to the light, instead of falling to the ground like a dead sparrow, is only the last act in a lifelong quest of understanding. "I am" then seems to prevail over "I will die," that other great certainty of life, if we live "I am" in the light of the great "I am" of the Gospels. There is certainty in "I am" and certainty also in "I will die" but in "I am" prevailing over "I will die" there is only understanding that comes of "Light,—more light!" in living and in dying, and the inner certainty of faith "seeing light with your heart when all your eyes see is darkness." If we do believe, we enter into the relationship of Jesus with the unknown and we too can call the unknown *thou* and Abba.

Returning to the Human Circle

"Light,—more light!" When I come back from my own solitude to speak to others, teaching "Things are meant" and "There are signs" and "The heart speaks" and "There is a way," I am speaking out of the light I have received, and I am always praying for "Light,—more light!" Maybe that is what Christ was doing, coming back from the desert to teach and yet returning to desert places again and again to pray. "Light,—more light!" is a prayer of one who teaches. I am relating to others in teaching them, but I can feel my own aloneness and my longing for "I and thou" which seems to have fulfillment only in "I and thou" with God, in love of God, in joy at the thought of God. I think again of Spinoza's words, "But all things excellent are as difficult as they are rare."[25]

A trust in divine providence, to be sure, is not as lonely as an impersonal God, for it means not only letting be but also being open to the mystery of encounter. When Jesus comes back from the desert, he meets those who are to be his disciples, and he says "Follow me!" Here is the mystery of encounter, the meaning hidden in the chance meeting. "Now they had to trust each other," we can say here too, "or else the world, transformed by their chance meeting, would become a place without meaning or future after all, a place merely of chance."[26] He had to trust his disciples, and they had to trust him, even though, as it turned out, one of them was to betray him. There wasn't the same mutual trust, though, when it came to the crowds that gathered to listen to him. John says "but Jesus did not trust himself to them, because he knew all men, and needed no one to bear witness of man; for he himself knew what was in man."[27]

To trust, then, means to entrust oneself. Jesus entrusts himself to Abba, his God, and also to his disciples but not to the crowds. And trusting comes of knowing: he entrusts himself to Abba, his God, because he knows Abba, and he trusts himself to his disciples because he knows his disciples. "I know whom I have chosen,"[28] he says even when revealing that one of them is to betray him. So trust, even his knowing trust, can be betrayed. He doesn't entrust himself to the crowds, though, because he knows what is in them. He shares with his disciples the secrets of the kingdom of God, while to the crowds all is in parables. Yet that may mean, as we said, simply that the secrets of love remain secret even when they are revealed, as Ramon Lull says, since only those who love will understand them. So Jesus shares the secrets of the love of God with his disciples, but these secrets are riddles to the crowd. Thus it is again, "all things excellent are as difficult as they are rare."

And yet these excellent and difficult and rare things are revealed to those who have the heart of a child. "I thank thee, Father,

Lord of heaven and earth, that thou hast hidden these things from the wise and understanding and revealed them to babes," Jesus exclaims; "yea, Father, for such was thy gracious will."[29] So Jesus finds followers among the simple folk and among the outcasts, the prostitutes and the publicans, rather than among the learned. I suppose this is because the secrets he is revealing are the secrets of love.

All the same, the secrets of love he is revealing "to babes" are excellent and difficult and rare, and to know them is to become great in love like the sinful woman who "loved much."[30] I think of Stephen Spender's poem where he says "the truly great" are those who "remembered the soul's history," "whose lovely ambition was . . . [to] tell of the Spirit," "who hoarded . . . the desires falling . . . like blossoms," "who in their lives fought for life," "who wore at their hearts the fire's centre."[31] All these things, I believe, belong to living in the great circle of love that comes from God and goes to God. Coming out of this great circle, Jesus comes into the human circle to call people out again into this great circle of love. Remembering the soul's history, I mean, is remembering how the love is *from God,* telling of the Spirit is telling how it is *of God,* and hoarding the desires falling like blossoms is realizing we are in love and the love is *toward God.* Fighting for life in life is fighting for life that is light and love, and wearing at your heart the fire's center is being caught up in the love that moves the sun and the stars.

Coming out of the great circle of the love of God, Jesus has to be willing to walk alone in the human circle. "He was already willing, we may note, to go alone," as Helen Luke says of one of Tolkien's characters, "would ask no one else to share the danger. In this perhaps is a clue to the fate which had chosen him. He was that rare thing, a man willing to walk alone."[32] It is by wearing at your heart the fire's center that you become able to walk alone, it seems, and it is willingness to walk alone that makes a human relationship heart-free. If I am willing to walk alone, I am able to let others be and be open to the mystery of our encounter. And if others turn toward me, I am able to welcome their companion-ship, and if others turn their back on me, I am able also to let them go.

Carrying the divine presence for others can leave you very alone and lonely, if you are the one carrying it. I see us carrying life for one another, carrying for example the mysterious life of the Spirit, and we have to be willing to do this for each other. And I see Jesus too carrying something like this for others, and I see his willingness to walk alone as a willingness to carry for others the presence of God. We have the story of Jesus as told in the Gospels by his disciples, by those for whom he carried the divine presence, and not as told by himself. If we try to pass over from the stand-point of the disciples to his own standpoint, we come upon this willingness to walk alone and to carry the Shekinah, the divine presence. Or so it seems to me, and that is why his retirement for solitary prayer, so emphasized in "The Harmony of the Gospels," is essential to his life. I don't mean by this to invalidate the stand-point of the disciples. Their perceptions of him, I want to say, are true. He does carry for them and for us the presence. God-with-us is who he is for us, and in this we encounter the mystery of the incarnation.

From his own point of view he stands in an "I and thou" with God, calling God "thou" and Abba. "God does not play dice," Einstein's saying, is true also from his point of view, though not perhaps in the way Einstein meant it. What would be a play of dice from the standpoint of "I and it," a chance meeting, has meaning from that of "I and thou." And so too a whole life story, relatively insignificant from the standpoint of "I and it," can be very signifi-cant from that of "I and thou." To say he is the Son of God would be a metaphor in terms of "I and it," but it is essential truth in terms of "I and thou," "for it is the *I* of unconditional relation," as Buber says, "in which the man calls his *Thou* Father in such a way that he himself is simply Son, and nothing else but Son."

"Everything is situated," Max Jacob says in his preface to *The Dice Cup*, his prose poems. "Everything that's above matter is situated; matter itself is situated."[33] To say I am situated is to say I stand in an "I and it" relation to my situation. To say Jesus himself is situated is to say he too stands in an "I and it" relation to his situation. This was the stumbling block for his contemporaries, "Yet we know where this man comes from," as they say in the Gospel of John, "and when the Christ appears, no one will know where he comes from." And Jesus answers "You know me, and you know where I come from? But I have not come of my own accord; he who sent me is true, and him you do not know." He is answering out of his "I and thou" with God, "I know him, for I come from him, and he sent me."[34] In terms of his "I and it" with his situation he is Jesus of Nazareth; in terms of his "I and thou" with God he is the Son of the Living God. This is the mystery of the incarnation, the conjunction between the "I and it" that situates him in time and place and the "I and thou" with God wherein he comes from God and goes to God.

Out of this mystery comes his teaching of the earth as a path that leads to the sky. We are situated on the earth but we are called into a relation with our Father who is in heaven. That saying of Jesus that is remembered among Muslims sums it up perfectly, "This world is a bridge: pass over it, but do not build your house on it."[35] Although I keep quoting Spinoza on the love of God as joy at the thought of God, I realize the God of Spinoza is very different from the God of Jesus. The physical world and the mental world are aspects of God for Spinoza, "attributes" he calls them. For Jesus the physical world and the mental world, together "this world," are a bridge leading to God, who is spirit. God then is near and far for Jesus, near as spirit pervading all, far as beyond the world.

Life then is a journey with God, for God is near, and a journey towards God, for God is far. What if the physical and mental world were aspects of God, as Spinoza says, and yet you had an "I and thou" relation with God? Would the physical and mental world then not be a bridge leading to God's essence, which is Being? As though God had crossed over coming to us and now we must cross over going to God. So it would be true after all, "This world is a bridge: cross over it, but don't build your house on it." Build not on the "attributes" but on the "essence." This "I and thou," though, would it not be rather "I and it" with the essence? If God is truly "thou" and not just a personification, then "God is spirit," as Jesus says to the woman at the well, and God is not situated, "neither on this mountain nor in Jerusalem,"[36] and God's relations with us and with the world are spiritual relations, relations of knowledge and love, I mean, so what God knows and loves comes to be, and our relations with God too have to be spiritual, relations of knowledge and love. And so we cross the bridge by knowing and loving.

Near and far. I think of two scenes I witnessed in the Holy Land.[37] One was when I first arrived and was waiting in customs behind a woman and her children, and her husband came and picked up the little girl, about two years old, and the child was pinching his cheek and saying "Abba! Abba!" The other was when I was in the north, waiting for a train south, and I turned around and saw a little boy all by himself in a wide empty space, crying "Abba! Abba!" The one scene was of intimacy, the little girl pinching her father's cheek; the other was of distance, the little boy alone and crying out. Both were using that word Jesus used for God, "Abba." And they seemed to embody that double aspect, the near and the far, the near as when he exclaims "I thank thee, Father, Lord of heaven and earth, that thou hast hidden these things from the wise and understanding and revealed them to babes," and the far as when he exclaims on the cross, "My God, my God, why hast thou forsaken me?"

It is this relation with God as Abba, the relation of the Son to the Father, that makes us free, according to Jesus, "if the Son makes you free, you will be free indeed." Human bondage, as Spinoza says,[38] is due to the power of the emotions, and human freedom to the power of understanding. For Jesus human bondage is due to sin, "every one who commits sin is a slave of sin," and human freedom comes of knowing the truth, "If you continue in my word, you are truly my disciples, and you will know the truth, and the truth will make you free."[39] The question here is Pilate's question "What is truth?" If God is near and far, if God is spirit, then truth goes with spirit, with the worship of God "in spirit and in truth." To enter into the relation of Jesus with God is to enter into this worship, and just as God is not situated "neither on this mountain nor in Jerusalem," so living in a relation with God makes you free in relation to your situation. It makes you able to take loss for instance, the loss of someone or something you are attached to, as a release into transcendence, like a bird that is set free and able to fly.

There isn't in this thinking an ideal of autonomy, but freedom is rather in the ability to love, to love God above all. So human bondage is conceived here not as what impairs autonomy so much as what impairs the ability to love—for Spinoza the power of the emotions, for Jesus the power of sin. I can feel the power of the emotions in my attachment to someone or something I have lost, how my thoughts keep returning to my loss, sending me through phases of anger and phases of sadness. I can feel the power of sin rather more subtly in the direction that my attachment gives to my life, realizing "love is a direction,"[40] as Simone Weil says, a direction towards God, a direction that can set me free from my attachment and from my recurrent bouts with anger and with sadness.

It is love's direction that I learn by continuing in his word, and that is knowing the truth that sets me free. Is "the truth" here the truth of my life and the truth therefore of my relationships with persons and situations? Or is it the truth rather of the love that comes from God and goes to God? I can feel the power of understanding here when I see my life "under the aspect of eternity,"[41] as Spinoza says, and in the light of the love that comes from God and goes to God, letting go of the attachment that submerges me in time and opening my heart to the mystery of eternal love. I can see time's arrow from past into future transformed into love's direction from God and towards God. The truth of my life is subsumed in the truth of the gospel, the truth of coming from God and going to God. Letting be and being open to the mystery can free me from my attachment and plunge me into the great circle of love. Or rather, vice-versa, it is the sense of love's direction that enables me to let be and be open to the mystery.

"We are hindered by cleaving to time," Meister Eckhart says. "Whatever cleaves to time is mortal."[42] Cleaving to time, I take it, is being attached to all I have lost, living in regret of the past and fear of the future, holding on to all I have lost, though it is already gone, and fearing more loss, though it has not yet come. What I learn from the Sermon on the Mount, nevertheless, is not living in the present so much as living in the Presence. The wisdom sayings, I mean, cannot be separated from the "I am" sayings and the sense of "God-with-us." What enables me to let go of regret and fear is the sense that God is with me on my journey in time. I don't have to live then in denial of the past and the future but in a "Thanks!" taking the past as from God and a "Yes!" taking the future as towards God.

"Eternal life belongs to those who live in the present,"[43] Wittgenstein says, but reading the Sermon on the Mount I want instead to say *Eternal life belongs to those who live in the Presence.* It is those who live in the Presence who are able to say "Thanks!" and "Yes!" Also "Thinking is thanking,"[44] the mystic saying of the seventeenth century that Heidegger is always quoting, might be turned around here to "Thanking is thinking," for the "Thanks!" and "Yes!" that arise out of the sense of Presence is not simply feeling but thinking, and it does not immediately take away fear and sadness. Still, it gives a direction to life, love's direction, and even though "love is a direction and not a state of soul," it can eventually become a state of soul and can transform fear and sadness into desire and gladness, and then indeed *Thinking is thanking,* thinking becomes feeling, thinking becomes thanking. And this seems to happen over and over again in life, each time fear and sadness arise.

Living in the Presence, I come to a kind of recovery from loss, God takes my loss from me, I mean, "God-with-us" fills my emptiness. Jesus does speak of loss even in this earlier period before the death of John the Baptist, before the shadow of the cross falls upon his own life. "He who finds his life will lose it," he says in Matthew, "and he who loses his life for my sake will find it."[45] As I understand this, "The God of Loss. The God of Small Things"[46] of our experience gives way to "God-with-us." Or that is how it seems to me, living in the Presence and saying "Thanks!" and "Yes!"

Before the shadow of the cross falls upon his life, the teaching of Jesus is in this transition, I believe, from "The God of Loss. The God of Small Things" of our experience to "God-with-us." "You have heard that it was said . . . ," he says, "but I say to you. . . ."[47] Our experience is one of loss and small things. If instead of the common notion that everything that happens to us is the will of God, we see our experience in the light of an "I and thou" with God as Abba, then we are carried inwards from what is happening to us to what is going on in our hearts. So it is not loss and small things that matter but our relationship to loss and to small things. It is "the pure in heart" who are blessed, who are able to see God, those who live in an "I and thou" with God, and that is not hard to do if you believe in "God-with-us," for then "your faith has made you whole"[48] as Jesus is always saying to the people he heals.

It is faith in God-with-us that makes you whole, insofar as separation from God and from humanity is what makes you sick. "Loneliness is not the sickness unto death,"[49] Hammarskjöld says, for in loneliness the separation is felt and so is on the way to reunion. But separation itself is the sickness and is at its worst when it is not felt. So the woman with the issue of blood feels her separation and says to herself "If I may touch but his clothes, I shall be whole," and the blind man feels his separation and calls out "Jesus, son of David, have mercy on me," and the Samaritan leper who is cleansed feels his reunion after separation and falls down at Jesus' feet giving thanks.[50] It is those who in "the hardness of their hearts"[51] do not feel their separation and their need of healing who become his adversaries. It is faith versus unbelief in God-with-us that leads to the cross.

Facing Death

"Christianity 'outruns' the cross"[52] Roland Barthes says, meaning the reality of Christianity goes beyond its symbol, the cross. The Gospel too outruns the cross, we could say, in that the Gospel begins before the shadow of the cross falls upon the life of Jesus and continues on beyond the cross in his resurrection. All the same, if we compare the image of Christ on the cross with the rival image of Mithras slaying the bull of death, we can see the essential idea of going through death to life set over against the idea of conquering death. In the public life of Jesus there is an earlier period, as we have seen, in which the essential message is simply that of "God-with-us." I see the death of John the Baptist as the great turning point in the public life of Jesus, when the shadow of the cross begins to fall on the life of Jesus. I see this as a dividing point in reading the Gospel of Matthew starting at chapter fourteen, Mark starting in chapter six, and Luke starting in chapter nine. A good part, or even the better part of each gospel, comes after this turning point. God-with-us becomes God-with-us in life and in death.

If we push the comparison and contrast between the image of Christ on the cross, going through death to life, and that of Mithras slaying the bull, conquering death, we can say there is in the Gospel not only a way of life but also a way of death. The mystery of Christianity is that of God-with-us in life and in death. Yet what of the cry from the cross "My God, my God, why hast thou forsaken me?" It is the mystery of God-with-us in our deepest loneliness. There is a paradox here, God-with-us when God has apparently forsaken us. The mystery of Christianity, symbolized in the cross, is that of a passage through death to life. The essential thing, it seems, is *going through*, going through death to life, through suffering to joy. The ability to love is in the willingness to go through.

To conquer death, I suppose, is "to conquer myself rather than fortune,"[53] as Descartes says, to conquer somehow my fear of death. To go through death to life, on the other hand, is to take death as an event of life like birth, to go through the letting go of everyone and everything that is required of us in death in order to enter into a new relation with everyone and everything. I thought at one time that we could follow Christ into solitude and back again into the human circle, and when it came to facing death we could follow there too insofar as we face the prospect of death in our own lives. But I thought we could not actually follow him through death to life for the simple reason that we are still alive. I thought we could follow him through death only when we came to die ourselves. Then I read *The Death of Ivan Ilych* by Tolstoy, and when I saw how death meant letting go of everyone and everything as Ivan Ilych is compelled to do on his deathbed, then I realized we too could go through death in the midst of life whenever we are compelled to let go of everyone and everything. And we can come thereby into a new relation with everyone and everything, "In place of death there was light."[54]

It is true, this story of letting go of everyone and everything runs counter to our cultural alienation from death, to "Death is not an event of life. Death is not lived through."[55] If we let ourselves be carried beyond alienation, nevertheless, then we have two moments here, one in which life opens up before us all the way to death, as it apparently did for Christ at the death of John the Baptist, and the other in which we go through death to life with him by letting go of everyone and everything.

"Night is drawing nigh," Hammarskjöld writes in his diary at the beginning of several of the later years of his life, as Jesus says "the night cometh"[56] in the Gospel of John at the prospect of his death. If I face with him my own night drawing nigh, I find myself facing it in his terms. If I were to face it in my own terms, I would be asking myself as I have in the past, "If I must die someday, what can I do to fulfill my desire to live?"[57] Facing it in his terms, I am facing it in terms of an "I and thou" with God as Abba. My own question arises in conversation with myself; his arises in conversation with God. My question is posed in terms of time's arrow from the past into the future. His question, I gather, is posed in terms of love's direction, the great circle of love coming from God and going to God. His question occurs in the Gospel of John. "Now is my soul troubled," he says. "And what shall I say? Father, save me from this hour? No, for this purpose I have come to this hour. Father, glorify thy name." And then the answer comes, a voice from heaven saying "I have glorified it, and I will glorify it again."[58]

Fear and sadness make it difficult to trust God, fear of what may happen, sadness at what has happened. It is the great circle of love that enables us to trust. "God does not play dice" and similarly God does not play chess, I want to say, but "The love is from God and of God and towards God." Death then is returning to God. If I believe in the great circle of love, then I become caught up in it, and my life is from God and of God and towards God. This is how I see myself entering into the "I and thou" of Jesus with God in the face of death. "Now is my soul troubled," he says in John, and "My soul is sorrowful, even to death,"[59] he says in Mark and Matthew in the Garden of Gethsemane. So he feels the fear and the sadness. To trust God in the face of fear and sadness I have to believe, like him I believe, in the great circle of love as the real meaning hidden in events rather than a dice game or a chess game.

"Oh, dear God, help your child to go on,"[60] the child prays in *Dear Mili*, a fairy tale by Grimm but discovered only in recent years. That is what I pray as I feel the fear and the sadness, I pray to go on with the great circle of love, and like the child in the story, my heart feels lighter. Even though the words are from a fairy tale, there is a profound truth here: God is not over and against us, God is with us. So it is the name of God-with-us that is glorified in our going through, for God is with us in our going through. The fear and the sadness of the prospect of death too, before we actually go through, is alleviated somewhat by the sense that God is with us. "Just as she expected, she felt lighter at heart," Grimm continues. "Rain began to fall, and she took comfort and said 'God and my heart are weeping together.'" I can say that, "God and my heart are weeping together," if I can say "God is vulnerable" and things can happen that are against the will of God but God is with us in those things and God's will for us in those things is our going through with love. Our going through then becomes part of the great circle of love.

"In the old times, when it was still of some use to wish for the thing one wanted,"[61] Grimm says at the beginning of one of his fairy tales. And that seems very pertinent here, if it is still of some use to pray for the thing I want. Christ himself prays for the cup to pass, and I can pray to be delivered from death. But the answer even to Christ himself is "No" or rather "I am with you." Of what use then was it for him to wish for the thing he wanted, or for me to wish for the thing I want? I suppose praying for the thing he wanted, for the thing I want, is of use in that praying is living in the "I and thou" with God, and is of use even when the "it" requested is denied, for by praying time's arrow, as it appears in the wishing and the wanting, is turned into love's direction.

We perish because we "cannot join the beginning to the end,"[62] as Alcmaeon, an early Greek philosopher, said, or perhaps we should say rather that the task of dying is to join the beginning to the end and that is what Christ is doing in laying down his life. The great circle of love is formed when we join the beginning to the end, when we join the "Thanks!" going back to the beginning to the "Yes!" going all the way to the end. I think of the final sentence of *The Death of Virgil*, "it was the word beyond speech," as if to say "In the end was the Word" as the Gospel of John begins "In the beginning was the Word." The great circle of love, though, passes through this world of darkness, of fear and hatred, "and the light shines in the darkness," and the darkness seeks to overshadow the light, and that is why the death of Jesus is what it is, death on a cross, and yet "the darkness has not overshadowed it," for as he says in the Gospel of John, "When you have lifted up the Son of man, then you will know that I am."[63] So the eternal Word is pronounced in the end as in the beginning, and the Word is "I am."

"To all that shall be—Yes!" is what Jesus is saying in the Garden of Gethsemane when he says "not as I will, but as thou wilt" in Matthew, or "not what I will, but what thou wilt" in Mark, or "not my will, but thine, be done" in Luke.[64] I think of the words in the Talmud, "for against your will you were fashioned, against your will you were born, against your will you live, against your will you die," or perhaps the right translation is "for without your will. . . ."[65] At any rate, when Jesus says "Yes" to the will of God, the "Yes" backs up from death to life to being born to being fashioned or conceived. And so the "Yes" becomes "Thanks," "For all that has been—Thanks!" and the "Yes" that goes all the way to the end is joined to the "Thanks" that goes back to the beginning.

Or this is how I understand the joining of the beginning to the end in the great circle of love, "Thinking is thanking." The thanking here in facing death takes place at the Last Supper, "And he took bread, and when he had given thanks he broke it and gave it to them," according to Luke; "and he took a cup, and when he had given thanks, he gave it to them," according to Matthew and Mark.[66] And so doing what he did at the Last Supper has come to be called Eucharist, that is, "thanksgiving." "Do this in remembrance of me,"[67] he says in Luke, and so doing this is like saying "For all that has been—Thanks!" looking to the past. At the same time there is a looking to the future in his "Do this" and also in his saying "I shall not drink again of this fruit of the vine until that day when I drink it new with you in my Father's kingdom" in Matthew, or "until that day when I drink it new in the kingdom of God" in Mark, or "until the kingdom of God comes" in Luke.[68] So there is hope here and not just willingness, there is the life-giving combination of willingness and hope in his "Yes," reaching to death and beyond.

"Thinking is thanking" for me too in facing the prospect of my own death, or thanking is a way to combine willingness with hope as my life passes before me in thinking. If I can thank God for all that has been, then I can hope in saying Yes to all that shall be. "What may I hope?" again Kant's question. It is an open-ended hope, *esperance* more than *espoir,* a hopefulness that goes with the willingness of my "Yes." Facing death, I hope for eternal life, understanding eternal life as in the Gospel of John, a life that has already begun now in knowing Jesus and knowing the God of Jesus. My hope arises simply from the "I and thou" with God of my willingness, my "Yes," a "Yes" to Someone and not simply a resignation to Something.

It is the "I and thou" with God that sustains Jesus even on the cross when he cries out "My God, my God, why hast thou forsaken me?" For those words are words of prayer, the beginning of a psalm. My point is not that the psalm, Psalm 22, if you read it through, ends in hope, or that he recited the psalm on the cross, but simply that these words are words of prayer and not of cynicism or of unbelief, and so he lives in the "I and thou" with God even at this darkest moment. "If separation ever touches him," Buber says of Jesus in *I and Thou*, "his solidarity of relation is the greater; he speaks to others only out of this solidarity."[69] His "seven last words" too, spoken from the cross, are spoken out of this solidarity: forgiving his enemies, promising paradise to the thief, recommending his mother and his beloved disciple to one another, crying out his thirst, crying out his God-forsakenness, saying it was consummated, and commending his spirit into the hands of Abba, his God.

He lives and dies in the "I and thou" with God, and so he rises again, for the "I and thou" is eternal, and eternal life is in the "I and thou" with God. I suppose this reasoning is a little too easy, but it seems to be his own reasoning in those last debates, "the subtle questions"[70] at the end of his public career when he answers the Sadducees with the idea that God is the God of the living and all are alive to God. If I live in an "I and thou" with God, I am living in a hopefulness as well as a willingness, not hope for a specific "it" as if the relation were an "I and it" but simply the hopefulness of the "I and thou" itself, the hopefulness of a child-like trust in God. It is not easy to hold on to childlike trust as life goes on and the losses and disappointments of life tend to make faith collapse into a kind of resignation.

If I live in an "I and thou" with God, then God becomes my "thou," I am living in a personal relation with the eternal "thou."

So my hope is eternal life, but that is simply the relation itself, the hope to be in the relation. What I come to in the end, I am guessing, is something like the last sentence in *The Death of Virgil*, "it was the word beyond speech." When my hope is gone in the human relations I have set my heart on, *espoir*, I find my hopefulness, *esperance*, inarticulate by comparison with *espoir* but real nonetheless, expressible only in "the word beyond speech" or expressible in the language of prayer that is also the language of poetry. My faith does not collapse then into resignation, but my hope goes over into hopefulness. I take it this is what is happening at the end for Jesus himself, his hope for Israel goes over into a hopefulness that looks to God alone.

"It was the word beyond speech," or in speech it was "I am," the Word that was in the beginning. As I seek to let go of fear and of sadness and even of desire and to abide in the peace of the divine presence, the divine "I am," I am seeking to let go of things we can tell and to hold to "we can know more than we can tell." I am listening to God tell my story, I am practicing attention "the natural prayer of the soul." And the story God is telling me, it seems, is my life is a journey in time and God is my companion on the way. As I come to the end of the way in death, however, what God is telling me seems "the word beyond speech." And I, I say "Thanks!" and "Yes!" "Story is our only boat for sailing on the river of time," Ursula LeGuin says in one of her stories, "but in the great rapids and the winding shallows no boat is safe."[71]

"Infinite resignation," that is what Kierkegaard calls it when there is no hope left but only willingness. So even though "no boat is safe," I have to trust in God, I have to hope, knowing "if one does not hope, one will not find the unhoped-for, since there is no trail leading to it and no path."[72] Instead of trying to figure out God, Does God play dice? Does God play chess? Does God take everything away? I look to myself, Am I willing? Do I hope? Am I standing in faith or only in infinite resignation? I clarify my understanding of God by clarifying my understanding of myself, by seeing the difference between faith and infinite resignation, between "the knight of faith" and "the knight of infinite resignation" as Kierkegaard calls them in *Fear and Trembling*. I realize then that God wants faith, not just infinite resignation, that God offers hope, even "the unhoped-for," and not just suffering and death. If then I hope, hoping simply in the "I and thou" with God, hoping in eternal life, I will find the unhoped-for, as Christ hoped in the "I and thou," "Abba, into thy hands . . . ," and found the unhoped-for, his rising to new life.

It was unhoped-for at least to his disciples, "for as yet they did not know the scripture, that he must rise from the dead."[73] Heraclitus says of the unhoped-for "there is no trail leading to it and no path." Or is there? That is just what Christ is, I am seeing now, the way to the unhoped-for, and apart from him indeed "there is no trail leading to it and no path," but he leads to the unhoped-for, rising from the dead. "Is everything sad going to come untrue?"[74] Sam asks in Tolkien's trilogy, and that is what the unhoped-for is, or rather instead of the sad coming untrue it is going through sadness to joy, going through death to life. Christ then is the way through. For Christ himself it is his trust in Abba that leads to the unhoped-for, and for us following him it is Christ who is our way, but we follow by hoping as he hoped in the "I and thou" with God.

"Where is the dancing? Where is the way?"[75] Ursula LeGuin asks in a story of the unhoped-for where "there is no trail leading to it and no path." There is dancing there where the way is if we take Christ to be the way to the unhoped-for. I think of the ancient *Hymn of Jesus* and of the rather thin line from there to the dancing Shakers in recent times. A rather thin line, to be sure. And I, when I compose song and dance cycles, I write the words and the music but I leave the choreography to the dancer. What is the matter here? Is it the otherworldliness of Christianity that contrasts so with the dancing Hasidim of Judaism and the dancing Sufis of Islam? "This world is a bridge: pass over it, but do not build your house on it." Is it possible still to dance, to dance over that bridge?

Maybe the answer is in another question, "How can we know the dancer from the dance?"

> O body swayed to music, O brightening glance,
> How can we know the dancer from the dance?[76]

So when we ask "Where is the dancing? Where is the way?" the answer is in the dancer, the one who is the way. I think again of the contrasting images, Mithras slaying the bull, conquering death, and Christ dying on the cross, going through death to life. There is the dance of the matador with the bull, the dance with fear, overcoming one's fear of death, and there is the dance of the Son of Man, the dance with one's humanity, of willingness to die and yet hope to live, of infinite resignation and faith.

A willingness to die and yet a hope to live, that is indeed a dance, a willingness to walk alone and yet a hope of human companionship. It is Kierkegaard who speaks of dancing, speaking of faith and infinite resignation, but Rilke has a conception of going through sadness to joy that I find most helpful here. He says of sadness "the future enters into us in this way in order to transform itself in us long before it happens."[77] As I understand him, there can be a happening, a loss, that brings about the sadness in us, and that is what has already happened when we are sad, but the sadness itself is the seed of something that is still to come and that is joy, and so our sorrow passes into joy, "your sorrow will turn into joy,"[78] as Jesus says in John. I feel the sadness of loss and disappointment in my life, and that is what tempts me to collapse into infinite resignation, but if I stay with faith, with hope as well as willingness, the future transforms itself in me, the future of my journey with God, as I stand in willingness to walk alone with the Alone. I rise to life already in life and hope to rise also in death.

Presence

He comes to us as One unknown,
without a name, as of old, by the
lake-side, He came to those men
who knew him not. He speaks to
us the same word: 'Follow thou
me!' and sets us to the tasks which
He has to fulfil for our time. He
commands. And to those who
obey Him, whether they be wise
or simple, He will reveal Himself
in the toils, the conflicts, the suf-
ferings which they pass through
in His fellowship, and, as an inef-
fable mystery, they shall learn in
their own experience Who He is.

—Albert Schweitzer

These are the concluding words of *The Quest of the Historical Jesus*.[1] They have even been set to music.[2] For me, though, they do not adequately describe the presence of Christ among us. To come into the presence, I think, we have to enter into the relation of Jesus with his God, Abba. As long as we are standing over and against Jesus, even in an attitude of recognition, we are still out-side. Only when we enter into his relation with God, dwelling in its particulars, the name, the kingdom, the will, the bread, the for-giveness, the guiding and the guarding from temptation and evil, are we in him and he in us, "I in them and thou in me."

It is true, nevertheless, "he comes to us as One unknown" and says "Follow me" and "sets us to the tasks which he has to fulfil for our time," and it is true, "he commands." We follow him, though, and fulfill those tasks and obey his command essentially by enter-ing into his relation with God, and so we come to know the "One unknown," for the relation with God is the secret of the re-lation with others that he commands and is the secret of our self-relation, which is at the heart of our own inner healing. And so it is true, "he will reveal himself in the toils, the conflicts, the suffer-ings" which we "pass through in his fellowship, and, as an inef-fable mystery" we "shall learn in" our "own experience who he is." We learn who he is and who we are by entering into his relation with God and calling God Abba; we come to understand "I" in coming to understand "thou" by living in his "I and thou" with God. When we enter into his relation with God, he disappears from in front of us and we find ourselves in an intimacy with his God, or then again we disappear and he lives in us, and this is the "ineffable mystery."

Parousia, the word in Greek, means "presence" first of all and only then, as a second sense, "coming." I take it that the Parousia is what is being described in the last line of Matthew, "I am with you always, even unto the end of time."[3] It is first the presence of God-with-us and only then the Second Coming. It is essentially the presence of Christ among us, I mean, what we experience when we enter into his relationship with God and he is living in us and we are living in him. It is then also his coming at the end of time when the hidden presence becomes manifest. The presence is our experience of Christ risen from the dead: the resurrection means (1) that he is alive, and (2) that he lives in us. I don't mean to reduce his being alive to his living in us, but only to say that our own experience of his being alive is his living in us. "He was like light," Peter says in the novel *Quo Vadis,* "and like the happiness of our hearts."[4] To us he is the inner light, the Light Within, the Christ Within, as the Quakers say, and so for us too, even at this distance in time from the events of the gospel, he is like light and like the happiness of our hearts.

But is it true to see Christ as the inner light, the Light Within, the Christ Within? "The light shines in the darkness," John says in his prologue, "and the darkness has not overshadowed it." That is how I am reading the Gospel, but is such a reading true to the Gospel? "That Christ may dwell in your hearts by faith,"[5] Paul prays for the Ephesians. Is this the way Christ dwells in our hearts by faith, as the inner light of faith, where faith is seeing light with your heart when all your eyes see is darkness?

Reading, as Proust understands it in his little essay *On Reading,* is essentially letting the past become present by way of words, but if we think of reading with faith, it can mean letting eternity become present. "Faith is God sensible to the heart," Pascal's saying (*La foi est Dieu sensible au coeur*), can also describe a method of reading, letting God become sensible to the heart by way of words. It is God-with-us who becomes sensible to the heart in reading the Gospel. Something like this happens also in reading the Suras of the Koran and in reading the Buddhist Sutras such as the Diamond Sutra and the Heart Sutra, eternity becomes sensible to the heart. If "attention is the natural prayer of the soul," we pass over to the Suras by letting attention become prayer, as we have seen, and we pass over to the Sutras by letting prayer become attention. As Malebranche understood it, though, in this saying, attention is to the inner light of faith in Christ, not that we can actually see the inner light but that we see things and situations in the light.

So I see, for instance, the death of a friend in this light, "One who believes in me, though he die, yet shall he live, and whoever lives and believes in me shall never die." My friend has died but I know that my friend lives, "for I know that my redeemer lives" and the God of Jesus is "not God of the dead but of the living, for all live to him."[6] All are alive in the inner light, even the dead, and the inner light itself is the light of Christ who is alive and lives in us. That light, though I speak of knowing, is the light of faith, seeing life and light and love with your heart when all your eyes see is death and darkness and lovelessness. I am thinking of a friend who was blind and incapacitated (from MS) and who took her own life, and I am trusting in the mercy of God to receive her.

Passing over in reading can also take place in this light, as when I read in a time of emotional unrest to recover my inner peace, reading for instance Tolkien's trilogy with its pervading sense of life as a journey, or when I read to recover "the simplicity of vision," reading for instance the *Confessions* of Saint Augustine with his vision of the soul wandering away from God and returning to God with tears, or when I read "to know that we are not alone," reading for instance Broch's *Death of Virgil* to know that I am not alone in facing the prospect of death. Passing over to Tolkien or to Augustine or to Broch, I am entering into the vision of another, entering into the feelings, the images, the insights of another, but I bring the light of my own faith to the vision and see it in the light. For Augustine the light is universal, as in John "It was the true light that illumines everyone coming into the world."[7] It is universal, I want to say too, but the appropriation of it is personal in faith. It is universal, and so I am able to pass over to others, but it is also personal, and so I have to come back again to myself from passing over.

Coming back then to myself, I find the inner peace, I find "the simplicity of vision," I find knowing we are not alone comes of appropriating the inner light in faith. Without the inner light things are only things, situations are only situations. But then again we don't see the light itself, only things and situations in the light. So we have to pass over to others and come back to ourselves to find the peace, the simplicity, the knowing. When I enter into Tolkien's story of the journey, I become able to see my own life as a journey in time, and when I enter into Augustine's story of the soul, I become able to see how the love comes from God and goes again to

God in my own life, and when I enter into Broch's story of facing death, I become able to find the Word in the end as in the beginning. The peace comes of the sense of being on a journey, the simplicity of the sense of love's great circle, the knowing I am not alone of the sense of "the word beyond speech"[8] hidden in the darkness of death.

Divine reading (*lectio divina*) then is reading in the inner light of Christ Within. It is reading inspired by "the love of learning and the desire for God." It is loving God "with all your mind." When I think of "the love of learning" I think of my father and my mother's father, how they educated themselves apart from school by reading, and I think of the breadth and enthusiasm of their reading. When I think of "the desire for God," though, I think of the depth of reading and I think of Saint John of the Cross saying God spoke one Word and then kept silence,[9] and I find myself looking to the Gospel of John to find that one Word. And yet I don't abandon for that the breadth and the omnivorous enthusiasm I inherited from my father and my grandfather, for I see the Word at both ends of life, both "In the beginning was the Word" and in the end "it was the word beyond speech." So I see the Gospel of John as the essence of Christianity, but I see it also as a reading glass for reading all else.

What is more, I see a connection with music, even a unity of words and music. Songlines can be found in the Gospel, like the songlines traversing aboriginal Australia described by Bruce Chatwin, potential songs that can serve as guidelines in the journey of life. I have added a set of Songlines of the Gospel at the end of this book to illustrate the idea, a kind of lyrical commentary on the Gospel of John. I have also brought those questions to the Gospel that Chatwin raises in *The Songlines:* Why are we the most restless, dissatisfied of animals? Why do wandering people conceive the world as perfect whereas sedentary ones always try to change it? Why have the great teachers—Christ or the Buddha—recommended the road as the way to salvation? Do we agree with Pascal that all our troubles stem from our inability to sit quietly in a room?[10] The answer I find in the Gospels is the "I am" of Christ, the "I am" that is the Word in the Gospel of John, "I am" as if to say I am what you are seeking in your restlessness and your wandering and your inability to sit quietly where you are, I am the way.

It is a way of communion, "I in them and thou in me," and it seems to suppose a "heart always contemplating communion,"[11] as in my friend's motto in Bengali, *milon shadhonay mogno antore.* Such a heart reflects, it seems to me, the deep loneliness of the human condition and the longing in that loneliness, what I call "the heart's longing" or "the heart's desire." What we long for in our loneliness, what I long for, is what Martin Buber calls "I and thou," a human relationship, even a human relationship with God. And what we find in Christ is an "I and thou" with God that is open to us, "I in them and thou in me," Christ dwelling in us and God dwelling in Christ. As I understand it, his intimacy with God, calling God Abba is open to us, as when we pray "Our Father who art in heaven. . . ."

Is this really an answer to the deep loneliness of the human condition, to our yearning for union and communion? It is, I think, but it is an altogether spiritual answer. It is the way of pure relation. It is like the Hindu answer, "God dwells in you as you,"[12] only it is not just indwelling but "I and thou." And then again it is not just "I and thou" but indwelling, "I in them and thou in me." I remember a Hindu friend saying of God dwelling in you as you, "It cuts right through that terrible loneliness that separates us from one another." We could say the same of Christ dwelling in you as you. There is something encompassing about it, even though it is altogether spiritual, for spirit encompasses flesh, and "God is spirit," the concept of God in the Gospel of John, implies that God is pervasive. Spirit pervades flesh, even though it is set against flesh in the language of the Gospel, "It is the spirit that gives life, the flesh is of no avail." So too we can say it is the spirit that takes away loneliness, the flesh is of no avail against loneliness.

"If you only followed the parables," Kafka says, "you yourselves would become parables" and with that heart-free. Would you become heart-free of your loneliness? Kafka is thinking of becoming heart-free of your daily cares. To become heart-free of your loneliness would mean loneliness giving way to a sense of presence. It would mean the longing in your loneliness becoming love. I can see the parables of Jesus moving us in that direction, especially the main one, the Parable of the Sower. If I identify with the sower in the parable, sowing the seed of the word, then the parable does speak to the loneliness of giving without receiving. At least at one time that is how I felt and saw loneliness, as giving without receiving. What the parable seems to say is that the sower broadcasts the seed, letting it fall on different kinds of ground, that the sower does not have control over the seed's yielding or failing to yield, that the sower lets go of the seed in sowing it. Here, then, we have the two elements, letting be and openness to the mystery. The letting be is letting others be, letting the seed fall. The openness is to the mystery of encounter, to the mystery of the word in the human heart.

I take "the secrets of the kingdom" revealed in the parables to be what mystics like Ramon Lull call "the secrets of love,"[13] the secrets of the love of God. Thus the secrets remain secret even after they have been revealed except to those who love. To understand the love of God as it is understood in the parables we have to enter into the relation of Jesus with his God, Abba, to enter into his prayer as he taught his disciples to pray. The crucial thing seems to be forgiveness, releasing others from the past and being released oneself by releasing, "getting rid of what you haven't got,"[14] of the love you wanted and haven't got in order to discover the love you have. Then in the depths of your loneliness you discover the love of God, you find joy at the thought of God, at the thought of walking with God.

To have or not to have—there is an idea in the Gospels of getting rid not only of what you haven't got, releasing others from what you think they owe you, but also of what you have got, leaving all things and following Christ. Yet it is balanced by the equal and opposite idea of receiving everything back a hundredfold, really by the idea that "grace is infinite."[15] I take that sentence from Isak Dinesen's story "Babette's Feast," but I see the idea in the story of the rich young man invited to follow Christ where Christ speaks of the eye of a needle, of the hundredfold, and of God, that all things are possible to God. There is a divine abundance implied in the banquets described in the parables and in the actual events of the Gospel such as the marriage feast at Cana and the loaves and the fishes and the Lord's Supper, and the idea that "grace is infinite" seems implied, though it is actually stated only in John, " for it is not by measure that he gives the Spirit." And the divine abundance seems to mean that renunciation is not final but the road not taken in life somehow rejoins the road taken, and there is ultimately one road.

Where this one road goes is in a great circle from God and to God: "The love is from God and of God and towards God,"[16] as the old Bedouin said to Lawrence of Arabia. I see the great circle of love in the parables of love, the Parable of the Prodigal Son and the Parable of the Good Samaritan. The Prodigal Son leaves his father and goes into a far country, wasting all his substance, and then he comes back to his father with tears. It is the story of the soul wandering away from God and then returning to God with tears. The Good Samaritan also makes a circle in his journey, finding the wounded man by the road and tending to him, and then paying the innkeeper on his return for whatever expense the wounded man has incurred. It is the mystery of encounter with the other person on the great circle of the love that comes from God and returns to God.

We love, I believe, with a love we do not know, and traveling the great circle of love depends on coming to know the love. There is a kind of knowing, then, in the Gospels, knowing the love of God, that lies at the heart of the teachings of Jesus, for instance the Beatitudes in the Sermon on the Mount. It is especially here that we can compare his teachings with those of Gautama, the Buddha, for instance the Four Noble Truths ("All egocentric life is suffering. This suffering is caused by misknowing and its consequences.

There is a real freedom from this suffering. The path to that freedom is eightfold").[17] There is a great peace that comes when my heart is in accord with God's heart, "his will is our peace" as Dante says, and that peace is my criterion for finding the true path in life—a path without peace is a path without heart—and that great peace is the blessedness of the Beatitudes, "Blessed are the poor in spirit. . . ." There is a paradox, nevertheless, in the Beatitudes if we compare them with the Four Noble Truths, the paradox of blessedness in suffering. If my heart is in accord with God's heart, I am blessed, and I can experience the great peace, even in the midst of suffering.

I can feel the great peace in a time of loss and sadness, for instance, for there is in the peace a paradoxical combination of willingness and hope, a willingness to die and yet a hope to live, a willingness to walk alone and yet a hope of human companionship. Kierkegaard calls that willingness "infinite resignation," but he calls the combination of willingness and hope "faith."[18] The willingness is the recognition and acceptance of God's love for us, but the willingness and the hope together is our human repetition of divine love, our "Thanks!" for what has been, our "Yes!" to what will be.

Where is the hope, though, in that "Thanks!" and "Yes!"? There is a story by Jean Giono, *The Man Who Planted Trees,* which appeared originally under the title "The Man Who Planted Hope and Grew Happiness."[19] It suggests to me a way of reading the Parable of the Sower as a parable of planting hope and growing happiness. Giono makes a distinction between *espoir* and *esperance,* between a hope where the heart is set upon someone or something and a hopefulness where the heart is open to the unknown future. It is that open hope or hopefulness, I believe, that is implied in "Thanks!" and "Yes!" to God. It is the hope of eternal life, but eternal life is not something you can set your heart on like "health and love and money" (*salud amor y dinero*) in the song, but is the unknown mystery that opens up before us when life opens up before us all the way to death. Eternal life is the deeper life of knowledge and love that we live already in relationship to the God of Jesus and is seen as living on through death in ways we cannot yet imagine. Hopefulness is what is implied in letting be and being open to the mystery.

When Dag Hammarskjöld wrote in his diary, "For all that has been—Thanks! To all that shall be—Yes!"[20] he was at the turning point of his life, making the turn from will to willingness and from hope to hopefulness. It was essentially his response to the call of the Gospel, "Follow me." I find myself at that same turning point as I read the Gospel, called to let go of my own will and live in willingness to walk alone with God, to let go of false hopes and live in hopefulness open to the mystery of encounter. I do believe there is a dynamic at work here in this combination of willingness and hope where the willingness to walk alone leads into the mystery of encounter, the "Yes!" ever leading to a new "Thanks!"

There are turning points also in the life of Jesus, and these too appear to be moments of willingness and hope. They are the points where his life crosses that of John the Baptist: his withdrawal into solitude after being baptized by John, his return to the human circle after John is imprisoned, and his facing death after the death of John.[21] There is a divine call, "You are my beloved Son," experienced in the moment of baptism and then challenged, "Are you?" in his temptations in the solitude of the desert. "I am" is his response in willingness and hope. What is expressed in "I am," I have learned from my friend David Daube,[22] is the Shekinah, the divine presence. Jesus has to be willing to carry the divine presence for others. At the same time he has to trust in the divine presence in the face of doubt and disbelief. As David understands it, "I am" is not personal but transcendent. Jesus is not pointing to himself, saying "I am," but to the presence of God. All the same, as I understand it, "I am" conveys the divine presence in the person of Jesus, as in the usual translations "It is I" and "I am he," and this is the mystery of incarnation.

To carry the divine presence for others, God-with-us, that is what Jesus has to be willing to do, it seems, returning from solitude to the human circle and taking up the word from John the Baptist, now imprisoned, "The kingdom of God is at hand." It is at hand in his person, as he invites others into his relationship with God, and becomes himself the sower who sows the seed of the word. His life, up to this point, has a pattern similar to that of Gautama, the Buddha, withdrawal into solitude and return to the human circle, but the message he brings can seem quite opposite, the "I am" of the Gospel instead of the "no self" of the Dharma. The contrast is not so great, though, if we make a distinction between two senses of "I," the "I" that is linked with will, as when a child says "No" and "mine," and the "I" linked with willingness and the deep center of stillness in us surrounded by silence, the "I" we come to in the long journey from "No" and "mine" to "Yes" and "yours."

It is this deeper sense of "I" that connects with the "I am" of the Gospel, as when in facing death Jesus prays "Not my will but yours be done," passing from will to willingness and from hope to hopefulness. In this last turning point, facing death, Jesus goes through "the test of loneliness," as David Daube calls it, where "God left him to himself in order to know all that was in his heart."[23] Thus he is revealed, and we are revealed, and God is revealed on the cross. If we compare the image of Mithras killing the bull, conquering death or conquering the fear of death, with that of Christ on the cross, going through death to life, we can see the redemptive significance of his death. It is not his death by itself that is redemptive but his going through death to life, and it becomes redemptive for us when we enter into his relation with God, going with him through death to life. If we enter into his relation with God, then he is alive for us and he actually lives in us. This is how we know him risen from the dead.

"In place of death there was light"[24] we can say with Tolstoy of going through death to life. Here we can see the essential meaning of the three great metaphors of the Gospel of John, life and light and love, the life that is light, the light that is love, and the love that is from God and of God and towards God. Our own participation in going through death to life is by letting go of everyone and everything when it is required of us at the turning points of life, above all in the hour of our death, in order to enter into a new relation with everyone and everything. When I go through the loss in my life of someone or something, it is then that I participate in the dying and rising of Christ. The new life I come to, not the life I would have chosen, is my taste of the risen life. In place of death then, sheer loss, there is light, new life opening up before me. For even when I lose someone or something very important to me, my life is still a journey with God, and I find the presence of God filling the empty place, and so too when I go through death itself, I am like Enoch, who "walked with God; and he was not, for God took him."

"God requires the heart," as is said in the Talmud, and the heart requires God, and that is why the roads of life converge and there is ultimately one road. "Isn't it grand, isn't it good, that language has only one word for everything we associate with love—from utter sanctity to the most fleshly lust?" Thomas Mann says in *The Magic Mountain*. "The result is perfect clarity in ambiguity, for love cannot be disembodied even in its most sanctified forms, nor is it without sanctity even in its most fleshly."[25] Yet there are three words for love in Greek, I found reading the last chapter of the Gospel of John, and comparing the two words for love there with the word for love in Plato's dialogues. There is Eros, Plato's word for the heart's longing, that has the whole range Mann speaks of, from the most fleshly lust to utter sanctity, and there is Philia, friendship and even divine friendship in the Gospel of John, and there is Agape, the love of God that is God's own love. And the longing becomes the love by way of friendship, I want to say, and thus again the roads of life converge, and there is ultimately one road.

"He used to say there was only one Road," Frodo says of Bilbo in Tolkien's trilogy, "that it was like a great river: its springs were at every doorstep, and every path was its tributary."[26] I understand this in the context of storytelling: once all things were at one and we understood the language of other living beings, then the human race emerged and separated from other living beings, and then the individual emerged and separated—thus our loneliness, and now we look forward to the time when we will be reunited with one another and with all living beings. The one Road is that road of reunion with humanity and with all else. In the context of reading the Gospel I see it as meaning the road not taken in life will rejoin the road taken, that "grace is infinite," that "the road goes ever on and on" as Tolkien says and will not dead-end. And I see the road of reunion as "the road of the union of love with God."

This is "the narrow way of eternal life whereof Our Saviour speaks in the Gospel," according to *The Dark Night of the Soul,* "along which way the soul ordinarily passes to reach this high and happy union with God."[27] So it is a narrow way, and there are dark nights in traveling it, and yet all roads converge upon it, for it is a way of human wholeness, of loving God "with all your heart, and with all your soul, and with all your might," and as the Gospels add, "and with all your mind." It is remarkable, then, to see how the Gospels end, Matthew in presence ("I am with you always . . ."), Mark in fear and trembling (it has been said "the ending of Mark is the beginning of wisdom"),[28] Luke in ascension as he begins the Acts, and John in the unending story ("I suppose that the world itself could not contain the books that would be written"). I see in all of them a sense that "the road goes ever on."

I use that turn of phrase from Tolkien's song cycle, *The Road Goes Ever On.*[29] It carries a suggestion of eternal life, a road that does not dead-end but keeps opening up before us. "Eternal life belongs to those who live in the present,"[30] as Wittgenstein says, but reading the Gospel, I want to say *eternal life belongs to those who live in the presence.* Living in the presence, in the relationship of Jesus with his God, Abba, going with him through death to life, we find ourselves on a road that does not dead-end. It is a road that makes the great circle of love coming from God and returning to God. And if the love of God is simply joy at the thought of God, we find it when we find our life is a journey in time and God is our companion on the way.

Songlines of the Gospel

In the Beginning
In the beginning was the
   Word,
and the Word was with God,
and the Word was God.
This was in the beginning
   with God;
all came to be through this,
and without this nothing
   came
that ever came to be.
In this was life,
and the life
was the light of humankind,
and the light
shines in the darkness,
and the darkness
has not overshadowed it.

Cana of Galilee
And the Word was I am,
for Word became flesh

and flesh became Word,
matter became spirit,
water became wine,
and what of you and me,
my hour has not come
—still, whatever he says do,
but he does not entrust
himself to them,
he knows their heart
and needs not anyone
to tell him
what is in the human heart.

The Man Who Came by Night
Where from
and where unto
wind blows
where it will,
you hear the sound,
you cannot tell
where from
and where unto,

and so of you
if born of spirit,
for the love
is from God,
and of God,
and towards God.

The Woman at the Well

Give me to drink
and I'll give you to drink
of water welling up
    eternally,
for God is spirit
breathing on our waters,
and God acts spiritually,
illumining our minds
and kindling our hearts,
and these waters of life
I give and take
are of the inner sea
you hear murmuring
when you listen
to your inmost self.

Doing What God Is Doing

Do you want to be healed?
See and say and do
what God is doing—
God is still at work
and not yet resting
in eternal sabbath,
for we are still in the sixth day
when God makes us human
    beings,
and we work along with God.

So I do nothing of my own
    accord
but only what I see God
    doing—
See what God is showing!
Say what God is telling!
Do what God is doing!

The Bread of Heaven

Give us today
our daily bread,
bread of the morrow,
of the Coming One,
the bread of heaven,
for whoever eats this bread
will live and will live
on through death,
will live on God
the living and undying.
Give us today
our daily bread,
bread of the morrow,
of the Coming One.

Where Are You From?

We can know more
than we can tell
of God unknown,
and you can know
and cannot tell
where I am coming from,
but if there is one
who can understand,
not only know
but understand,

then I am unalone
and I can tell
of God unknown,
and God is here with us.

Where Are You Going?
If you follow me,
you will not walk in darkness,
you will have the light of life,
but if you are not with me,
you will never come
where I am going,
going back to God,
my going like my coming,
but if you continue in my
    word,
you will know truth,
and truth will make you free,
the children of the man
who trusted God,
and not the children of
    mistrust.

Blind and Seeing
If the blind
lead the blind,
all fall down
into the pit,
but if the seeing
lead the blind,
then give us light
and we will walk
into the dark,
and if the blind
lead the seeing,

we will walk
and will find light
instead of dark.

The Good Shepherd
O Lord, go with me
and be my guide,
in my most need
be by my side:
if you are guiding me
I shall not want,
if you are guarding me
I shall not fear,
though I am walking
in the valley of the shadow
of my dying,
you are walking with me,
and when I am not
you will have taken me.

I Am Resurrection
If you walk in light
you will not stumble
for you have the light within,
but if you walk in darkness
you will stumble
for there is no light in you,
and if you sleep
I will awaken you,
for I am resurrection, I am life,
if you believe in me
though you are dead
yet shall you live,
and if you live and you believe
in me you shall never die.

The Hour

Now that the hour has come
that I be lifted up from earth
and draw all others to myself,
my soul is troubled
and what shall I say,
my God deliver me
from evil in this hour?
Yet to meet the evil
have I come into this hour,
Father glorify your name
by being Father to me
as I am your child,
for I know your will for me
is eternal life.

A New Command

I know my time has come
to leave this world
and to return to God
as I have come from God,
and I know you
whom I have chosen,
and I have loved you
although I know of your denial
and betrayal of my love,
still I give you a new
    command,
to love as I have loved you
and to know as I have known,
to know your origin
and to know your return.

Eternal Return

Let not your heart be troubled:
you believe in God,
believe also in me,
for there are many places
in my Father's house
as there are in the human
    heart,
and I go to prepare a place
    for you,
and I will come again
and take you to myself,
so where I am
there you will be,
and you know where I go,
you know the way
by knowing God in me.

Abide in Me

Abide in me
and I in you,
let my God be your God,
and you will be like me
and you will be inside,
and you will be to me
not as my servants
but as friends,
for servants are outside
and do not understand,
but you friends are inside
and you shall understand
the love that comes from God
and goes again to God.

Proving the Unseen

Sorrow fills your heart
as I am leaving you,
but it is better that I go,
for if I never leave

the Spirit never comes,
but if I go it comes
by proving the unseen,
the mystery that shows
and then withdraws,
as for a little while
you shall not see me,
and again a little while
and you shall see me,
and your sorrow will turn
   to joy.

Lord's Prayer
O Father who in heaven
are Father to me
as I am Son to you,
be Father also
to those you have given me,
keep them as I have kept them
all one in your name
and in your kingdom come
and your will done on earth,
for I have given them
your word to eat as bread
and kept them from all evil,
I in them
and you in me.

I am / I am not
I am,
I am he,
it is I
whom you are seeking,
for *I am* is presence,
is my presence,
is the presence of my God,

but if I am
then let these others go
who have only to say
I am not,
I am not he,
it is not I
who am.

I am / I will die
Am I a king?
My kingdom
is not of this world,
I have come
to bear witness
to the truth.
What is truth?
Where am I from?
I am
and I will die:
Behold your son!
Behold your mother!
and I thirst
and It is finished.

Seeing and Believing
Faith is seeing light
with your heart
when all your eyes see
is darkness
—see and do not cling
for I am rising
to my Father
and your Father,
to my God and your God
—you see me
and you believe,

blessed are those
who see not with their eyes
but only with their heart.

Do you love me?
Do you love me?
Yes, Lord,
I am your friend.
But do you *love* me?
Yes, Lord,

I am your friend.
Are you my friend?
Lord, you know all things,
you know I am your friend.
Then follow me—
when you were still young
you chose your freedom,
but when you are old
you will have to *choose
    necessity.*

NOTES

Preface

1. John T. Frederick and Leo L. Ward, *Reading for Writing,* 3rd ed. (New York: F. S. Crofts, 1946).

2. See below "On Reading," note 24.

3. See below "On Reading," note 37.

4. See below "Turning Points," note 54.

5. See below "Parables," note 97.

6. Albert Schweitzer, *The Quest of the Historical Jesus* (Baltimore and London: Johns Hopkins University Press, 1998), p. 398 ("There is nothing more negative than the result of the critical study of the Life of Jesus.")

7. Ascribed to Aquinas in George N. Shuster, *Saint Thomas Aquinas* (New York: Heritage, 1971), p. 3.

On Reading

1. William Nicholson is the author of both the play, *Shadowlands* (New York: Penguin, 1991), and the screenplay (1994), but this line occurs only in the screenplay.

2. Marcel Proust, *On Reading,* trans. John Sturrock (New York: Penguin, 1994), p. 27.

3. Mary Stewart, *Merlin Trilogy* (New York: William Morrow, 1980).

4. See my discussion in *The House of Wisdom* (San Francisco: Harper & Row, 1985, rpt. Notre Dame, Ind.: University of Notre Dame Press, 1993) where these four sentences are chapter titles.

5. T. E. Lawrence, *Seven Pillars of Wisdom* (Harmondsworth, England: Penguin and Jonathan Cape, 1971), p. 364. See my discussion in *The Reasons of the Heart* (New York: Macmillan, 1978; rpt. Notre Dame Press, 1979), p. 1.

6. Dante, *Paradiso* 33: 143–45 (my translation). I am using the edition by E. Moore and Paget Toynbee, *Le Opere di Dante Alighieri* (Oxford: Oxford University Press, 1963), p. 153.

7. Arthur J. Arberry, *The Koran Interpreted* (Oxford: Oxford University Press, 1964), p. xii.

8. Homer, *The Odyssey,* trans. W. H. D. Rouse (New York: Penguin/ Mentor, 1937), p. 126.

9. See my book *The Homing Spirit* (New York: Crossroad, 1987; rpt. Notre Dame Press, 1997), p. 2 (I met this Sufi sheik on my second pilgrimage to Jerusalem, in 1976).

10. I am quoting Arberry's translation of the opening invocation of each Sura of the Koran and Edward Conze's translation of the opening invocation of the Diamond Sutra and the Heart Sutra in his *Buddhist Wisdom Books* (London: Allen & Unwin, 1958), pp. 21 and 77.

11. Peter Matthiessen, *The Snow Leopard* (New York: Viking, 1978), pp. 209–10.

12. See Richard F. Burton, *The Arabian Nights* (New York: Triangle, 1932), p. 1 and N. J. Dawood, *Tales from the Thousand and One Nights* (New York: Penguin, 1973), p. 13.

13. This was a Buddhist-Christian dialogue on "Models of Education" sponsored by the Fetzer Foundation at Kalamazoo, Michigan on July 11–14, 1996.

14. See my discussion of this saying in *Love's Mind* (Notre Dame: University of Notre Dame Press, 1993), pp. 86–87. See below, note 28 for references.

15. Matthiessen, *The Snow Leopard*, p. 247.

16. See my book, *The House of Wisdom,* p. 123.

17. Conze, *Buddhist Wisdom Books,* p. 68.

18. Ibid., pp. 101–2.

19. Arberry, *The Koran Interpreted*, pp. 356–57 (Koran 24:35).

20. Dawood, *Tales from the Thousand and One Nights,* p. 184.

21. Nicolas Cusanus, *Of Learned Ignorance*, trans. Germain Heron (New Haven, Conn.: Yale University Press, 1954).

22. See Rudolf Otto, *Mysticism East and West*, trans. Bertha L. Bracey and Richenda C. Payne (New York: Meridian, 1958) and Frithjof Schuon, *The Transcendent Unity of Religions*, trans. Peter Townsend (New York: Pantheon, 1963).

23. Simone Weil, *Waiting for God*, trans. Emma Craufurd (New York: Harper & Row, 1951). See especially her essay on studies, pp. 105–16.

24. Dag Hammarskjöld, "A Room of Quiet: the United Nations Meditation Room" (New York: United Nations, 1971), opening sentence.

25. Louis Massignon, *The Passion of Al-Hallaj*, trans. Herbert Mason, vol. 1 (Princeton: Princeton University Press, 1982), pp. 126–34.

26. Hammarskjöld, "A Room of Quiet," concluding sentence.

27. Massignon, *The Passion of Al-Hallaj*, p. L (1921 Foreword).

28. Nicolas Malebranche, *Oeuvres*, ed. Genevieve Rodis-Lewis and Germain Malbreil (Paris: Gallimard, 1979), vol. 1:1132 (my translation).

29. See his preface, ibid., p. 4.

30. John 6:44–46 (RSV)

31. Arthur Zajonc, *Catching the Light* (New York: Oxford University Press, 1993), p. 2.

32. Saint Augustine, *Confessions*, trans. Henry Chadwick (Oxford: Oxford University Press, 1991), p. 265 (*Confessions* 12: 25).

33. Diogenes in *Herakleitos and Diogenes*, trans. Guy Davenport (San Francisco: Grey Fox, 1983), p. 47 (aphorism # 47).

34. My translation of *noverim me, noverim te*. See *The Soliloquies of Saint Augustine*, trans. Rose Elizabeth Cleveland (Boston: Little, Brown, 1910), p. 51 (Book II, chapter 1) (she translates "let me know myself, let me know Thee!").

35. My translations of John 21:15 ff. I am using the Greek text edited by Nestle, *Novum Testamentum Graece et Latine*, rev. by Erwin Nestle and Kurt Aland (Stuttgart: Wurtembergishce Bibelanstalt, 1963) (22nd edition).

36. See Plato's *Symposium* trans. Percy Bysshe Shelley (New York: Peter Pauper, no date).

37. Hermann Broch, *The Death of Virgil*, trans. Jean Starr Untermeyer (San Francisco: North Point, 1945), p. 482.

38. John 6:68 (RSV).

39. John 7:16–17 (RSV).

40. Dante, *Paradiso* 3: 85 in Toynbee, p. 107.

41. Martin Heidegger, *Discourse on Thinking,* trans. of his *Gelassenheit* (including "A Conversation on a Country Path") by John M. Anderson and E. Hans Freund (New York: Harper & Row, 1966), p. 62.

42. Ibid., p. 60.

43. Ibid., p. 69.

44. Ibid., p. 70.

45. Ibid., p. 82.

46. Ibid., p. 71.

47. Rainer Maria Rilke, *Letters to a Young Poet,* trans. M. D. Herter Norton (New York: Norton, 1954), p. 35.

48. Michael Polanyi, *The Tacit Dimension* (Gloucester, Mass.: Peter Smith, 1983), p. 4.

49. Pierre Rousselot, *L'intellectualisme de Saint Thomas* (Paris: G. Beauchesne, 1924), p. 109 (my translation). See my discussion of this in *The House of Wisdom,* p. 89 and note 24 on p. 93.

50. Martin Buber, *I and Thou,* trans. Ronald Gregor Smith (New York: Scribners, 1958), pp. 66–67.

51. Galatians 2:20 (KJ).

52. Romans 8:26 (RSV).

53. Søren Kierkegaard, *Fear and Trembling* (with *Sickness unto Death*), trans. Walter Lowrie (Garden City, N.Y.: Doubleday, 1954), p. 59.

54. Mark 6:50 and Matthew 14:27 (my translation).

55. See my conversation with David Daube reported in *The Peace of the Present* (Notre Dame: University of Notre Dame Press, 1991), pp. 93–95.

56. Christopher Norris and Andrew Benjamin, *What Is Deconstruction?* (New York: St. Martin's Press, 1988), p. 7.

57. See George Steiner, *Real Presences* (Chicago: University of Chicago Press, 1989), p. 99.

58. Matthew 1:22–23 (RSV).

59. Machiavelli, Letter to Francesco Vettori (December 10, 1513), trans. Allan Gilbert, *Machiavelli,* vol. 2 (Durham, N.C.: Duke University Press, 1965), p. 929. I have modified the translation slightly, cf. the original text in Machiavelli, *Opere,* ed. by Mario Bonfantini (Milan and Naples: Ricciardi, 1954), p. 1111. See my discussion in *The Way of All the Earth* (New York: Macmillan, 1972; rpt. Notre Dame Press, 1978), p. 157.

Divine Reading

1. Ursula LeGuin, *A Wizard of Earthsea* (Berkeley, Calif.: Parnassus, 1968), p. 85.

2. Saint Augustine, *Confessions* (trans. Chadwick), p. 121 (*Confessions* 7:9).

3. Goethe, *Faust*, trans. Bayard Taylor (New York: Modern Library, 1967), p. 43 (*Faust*, Part One, Scene 3).

4. Jean Leclercq, *The Love of Learning and the Desire for God*, trans. Catharine Misrahi (New York: Fordham University Press, 1982).

5. Michel Serres, *Genesis*, trans. Genevieve James and James Nielson (Ann Arbor: University of Michigan Press, 1995), p. 110.

6. Ibid., p. 13.

7. Ibid., p. 7.

8. John Cage, *Silence* (Hanover, N.H.: Wesleyan, 1973), p. 3.

9. Serres, *Genesis,* p. 138.

10. 1 John 1:1 (my trans.).

11. Albert Schweitzer, *The Quest of the Historical Jesus,* Montgomery, pp. 370–71.

12. John 1:1–5 (my trans.).

13. Peter Levi, *The Holy Gospel of John* (Wilton, Conn.: Morehouse-Barlow, 1985), p. 7.

14. Matthew 28:20 (my trans.).

15. See my discussion of the *Ave Verum* in my book *The Music of Time* (Notre Dame, Ind.: University of Notre Dame Press, 1996), pp. 107–17.

16. Josquin Desprez, *In Principio Erat Verbum* in A. Smijers, ed., *Werken van Josquin Des Prez,* vol. 14 (Amsterdam: Alsbach, 1954), pp. 106 ff.

17. Luther as quoted by Jeremy Noble in his article on Josquin in *The New Grove Dictionary of Music and Musicians,* ed. by Stanley Sadie (London: Macmillan, 1980), 9:723.

18. Jeremy Noble in his article on Josquin, ibid., p. 722.

19. John Adams, *China Gates* (1977) and *Phrygian Gates* (1977–78) (New York: Associated Music Publishers, 1983).

20. Heidegger, *Early Greek Thinkers,* trans. David Ferrill Krell and Frank A. Capuzzi (San Francisco: Harper SF, 1984), p. 59 (my trans. of the Greek given there).

21. Ibid., p. 73.

22. Serres, *Genesis*, p. 4.

23. Pierre Teilhard de Chardin, *The Phenomenon of Man,* trans. Bernard Wall (New York: Harper & Row, 1959), and *The Divine Milieu,* trans. Bernard Wall (New York: Harper & Row, 1960).

24. J. R. R. Tolkien, *The Lord of the Rings* (London: Allen & Unwin, 1969), p. 540.

25. Thrasybulos Georgiades, *Greek Music, Verse and Dance* (New York: Merlin, no date), p. 153.

26. Paul Claudel, *Two Dramas,* trans. Wallace Fowlie (Chicago: Regnery, 1960), p. 298 (*The Tidings Brought to Mary,* act 4, scene 2). I have modified the translation slightly using the French text in Claudel, *Theatre* (Paris: Gallimard, 1965), vol. 2, p. 214. See my discussion in *The Peace of the Present,* pp. 43–44.

27. See J. S. Bell's critical presentation of the many worlds interpretation in his *Speakable and Unspeakable in Quantum Mechanics* (Cambridge: Cambridge University Press, 1987), pp. ix, 93–99, 117–38, and 192–93.

28. Proust, *On Reading,* p. 54.

29. See the interview with John Adams by Jonathan Cott, June 1985 with the Compact Disc recording of Adams' *Harmonielehre* (Nonesuch Digital, 1985).

30. Isidore of Seville quoted as epigraph to Marc Sebanc's novel *Flight to Hollow Mountain* (Grand Rapids, Mich.: Eerdmans, 1996), p. i.

31. Saint John of the Cross, *Collected Works,* trans. Kieran Kavanaugh and Otilio Rodriguez (Washington, D.C.: Institute of Carmelite Studies, 1979), pp. 179–80 (*Ascent of Mount Carmel* 2:22).

32. Beethoven, String Quartet in F Major, Opus 135, ed. Wilhelm Altmann (New York: Ernst Eulenburg, 1911), pp. ii and 20.

33. Proust, *On Reading,* pp. 53–54.

34. Plato, *Timaeus* 37d (my trans.).

35. Martin Buber, *Good and Evil,* trans. Ronald Gregor Smith and Michael Bullock (New York: Scribners, 1953), p. 43. See my discussion of this passage in *The Homing Spirit,* p. 65 and *Love's Mind,* p. 41.

36. Simone Weil, *Waiting for God,* p. 135.

37. Shakespeare, *I Henry IV,* act 2, scene 4, line 359 in The Pelican Shakespeare, ed. Alfred Harbage (Baltimore: Penguin, 1969), p. 685.

38. Tolkien, *The Lord of the Rings,* p. 73.

39. Ibid., p. 739.

40. Ibid., pp. 86–87.

41. Bruce Chatwin, *The Songlines* (New York: Penguin, 1987), pp. 161–62.

42. John 5:17 and 19 (RSV).

43. John 14:12 (RSV).

44. John 9:4 and 11:9–10 (RSV).

45. Dag Hammarskjöld, *Markings,* trans. Leif Sjöberg and W. H. Auden (New York: Ballantine, 1983), pp. 28 (1950), 50 (1951), 68 (1952), 74 (1953), 79 (1954), and 126 (1957).

46. Jean-Pierre de Caussade, *Abandonment to Divine Providence,* trans. John Beevers (New York: Doubleday, 1975).

47. Chatwin, *The Songlines,* p. 179.

48. George MacDonald, *The Golden Key* (New York: Farrar, Straus & Giroux, 1967), p. 34.

49. John 16:32 (RSV).

50. Robert Burton, *Anatomy of Melancholy,* ed. Floyd Dell and Paul Jordan-Smith (New York: Tudor, 1941), p. 970.

51. John 6:63 (RSV).

52. John 4:34 (RSV).

53. Reiner Schurmann, *Meister Eckhart* (Bloomington and London: Indiana University Press, 1978), p. xiv.

54. Kathleen Norris, *Dakota* (New York: Ticknor & Fields, 1993), p. 102.

55. Kant, *Critique of Pure Reason,* trans. Norman Kemp Smith (London: Macmillan, 1961), p. 635 (I have put "What should I do?" in place of "What ought I to do?").

56. John 5:6 (RSV).

57. From his poem "The Gift Outright" in *The Poetry of Robert Frost,* ed. Edward Connery Lathem (New York: Holt, Rinehart & Winston, 1969), p. 424.

58. Kierkegaard, *Purity of Heart Is to Will One Thing,* trans. Douglas V. Steere (New York: Harper, 1938).

59. Tolkien, *The Lord of the Rings,* p. 427.

60. John 12:50 (RSV).

61. Kierkegaard, *Repetition,* trans. Walter Lowrie (Princeton: Princeton University Press, 1946), p. 144.

62. John 4:13–14 (RSV).

63. Helen Luke, *Dark Wood to White Rose* (New York: Parabola, 1989), p. 165 (Dante, *Paradiso* 23: 46). This quotation from Dante is the epigraph of Charles Williams' study, *The Figure of Beatrice* (Cambridge: Brewer, 1994), p. 6.

64. Luke, *Dark Wood to White Rose*, p. 199 (Dante, *Paradiso* 33: 145).

65. Catherine Mowry LaCugna, *God for Us* (San Francisco: Harper SF, 1991) and her essay in the book she edited, *Freeing Theology* (San Francisco: Harper SF, 1993), p. 83.

66. John 14:8–9 (RSV).

67. Pascal, *Pensees* #481 in Pascal, *Oeuvres Completes,* ed. Jacques Chevalier (Paris: Gallimard, 1954), p.1222. See my discussion in *The Music of Time*, p. 132.

68. Heidegger, *Being and Time,* trans. Joan Stambaugh (Albany, N.Y.: State University of New York Press, 1996), p. xix.

69. Broch, *The Death of Virgil,* p. 43.

70. George MacDonald, *Phantastes* (New York: Ballantine, 1970), p. 129.

71. John 13:33 and 14:1–3 (RSV).

72. Henri Nouwen, *The Inner Voice of Love* (New York: Doubleday, 1996).

73. T. S. Eliot, *The Three Voices of Poetry* (New York: Cambridge University Press, 1954).

74. From a talk he gave on holiness, June 11, 1997, at Notre Dame.

75. John 15:11 (KJ).

76. Jean Giono, *Joy of Man's Desiring,* trans. Katherine Allen Clarke (San Francisco: North Point, 1980), and *The Man Who Planted Trees* (White River Junction, Vt.: Chelsea Green, 1985) originally published in Vogue (1954) as "The Man Who Planted Hope and Grew Happiness."

77. John 17:23 (RSV).

78. John 4:24 and 1 John 1:5 and 4:8 (RSV).

79. Compare Simone Weil, *Waiting for God,* and Samuel Beckett, *Waiting for Godot* (New York: Grove, 1956).

80. MacDonald, *The Golden Key,* p. 72.

81. Pierre Hadot, *Plotinus or The Simplicity of Vision,* trans. Michael Chase (Chicago: University of Chicago Press, 1993).

82. See the passages on "the hermeneutic circle" in Heidegger, *Being and Time,* pp. 7–8, 152–53, and 314–15 (page numbering from the German original as given in Stambaugh trans.).

83. John 8:12 (my trans.).

84. Nietzsche, *Beyond Good and Evil,* trans. Walter Kaufmann (New York: Random House, 1966), p. 89 (Book 4, aphorism 146).

85. Spinoza, *Ethics,* trans. G. H. R. Parkinson (London: Dent, 1989), pp. 210 and 218 (Book 5, propositions 19 and 36).

86. John 16:28 (RSV).

87. Novalis as quoted by Etienne Gilson, *God and Philosophy* (New Haven, Conn.: Yale University Press, 1941), p. 102.

88. Genesis 5:24 (NRSV).

89. See my discussion of the cycles of storytelling in *The Peace of the Present,* pp. 71–72.

90. See my discussion of this phrase in *Love's Mind,* p. 99.

91. From my translation of the poem of Saint John of the Cross, "Dark Night," in my book *Love's Mind,* p. 100.

92. John 14:5–6 (RSV).

93. John 15:4 (RSV).

94. Buber, *I and Thou,* pp. 66 and 85.

95. Ibid., p. 67.

96. John 12:24 (RSV).

97. John 16:7 (RSV).

98. John 12:32 (my trans.).

99. C. G. Jung, *Answer to Job,* trans. R. F. C. Hull (London: Routledge & Kegan Paul, 1954), pp. 93–94.

100. 1 John 1:5 (RSV).

101. John 12:27–28 (RSV).

102. Mark 15:39 (RSV).

103. Kafka, *The Great Wall of China,* trans. Willa and Edwin Muir (New York: Schocken, 1974), p. 183 (aphorism 101). Instead of "effort" I use the word "striving" from Nahum Glatzer's translation of the same passage in his *Language of Faith* (New York: Schocken, 1967), p. 35. See my discussion in *The Homing Spirit,* p. 39.

104. Paul Celan, *Collected Prose,* trans. Rosemarie Waldrop (New York: Sheep Meadow, 1986), p. 49.

105. Heidegger, *Discourse on Thinking,* p. 54.

106. Heidegger quoted by Reiner Schurmann in the epigraph of his *Meister Eckhart,* p. vii.

107. Heidegger, *Discourse on Thinking,* p. 55.

108. Ibid.

109. Buber, *I and Thou*, p. 63.

110. Dietrich Bonhoeffer, *Letters and Papers from Prison*, ed. Eberhard Bethge (New York: Macmillan, 1971), p. 234.

111. John 10:10 (RSV).

112. 1 John 1:3 (RSV) and 4 (KJ).

113. John 17:2 (RSV).

114. Heidegger, *Discourse on Thinking*, p. 82.

115. Hammarskjöld, *Markings*, p. 74.

116. Saint John of the Cross, *Collected Works*, p. 97 (*Ascent of Mount Carmel* 1:9).

117. Heidegger, *Discourse on Thinking*, p. 62.

118. John 6:38 (RSV).

119. Rudolf Bultmann, *Theology of the New Testament*, trans. Kendrick Grobel, vol. 2 (New York: Scribners, 1955), pp. 84–85.

120. Ephesians 3:17 (RSV).

121. Heidegger, *Discourse on Thinking*, p. 85.

122. Mimi Louise Haskins as quoted by George VI in a Christmas broadcast in 1939, *King George VI to His Peoples* (London: John Murray, 1952), p. 21.

Parables

1. Kafka, *Parables and Paradoxes*, trans. Heinrich Mercy Sohn (New York: Schocken, 1961), p. 11.

2. John 16:28–29 (RSV).

3. Matthew 8:20 and Luke 9:58 (RSV). The saying about the world as a bridge is discussed by Kenneth Cragg, *Jesus and the Muslim* (London: Allen & Unwin, 1985), p. 47, and by Joachim Jeremias, *The Unknown Sayings of Jesus*, trans. Reginald H. Fuller (London: SPCK, 1964), pp. 111–18. See my discussion in *The Peace of the Present*, p. 102.

4. Kafka, *Parables and Paradoxes*, p. 11.

5. Matthew 13:3–9 and 18–23; Mark 4:2–9 and 14–20; Luke 8:5–8 and 11–15.

6. John 4:37 (RSV).

7. John 4:38; Matthew 9:37; Luke 10:2.

8. Mark 4:13 (RSV).

9. Mark 4:11–12 (RSV).

10. Frank Kermode, *The Genesis of Secrecy* (Cambridge, MA: Harvard, 1979).

11. Mark 4:11; Matthew 13:11; Luke 8:10 (RSV). See the sayings where the word *secrets* occurs in the *Libre de Amic e Amat* (nos. 32, 75, 76, and 155) in Salvador Galmes and Miguel Ferra (eds.), *Obres de Ramon Lull*, vol. 9 (Palma de Mallorca: Comissio Editora Lulliana, 1914), pp. 383, 389, 390, and 400–1. See my discussion in *The House of Wisdom*, pp. 161–62.

12. Ramon Lull, *The Book of the Lover and the Beloved*, trans. E. Allison Peers (London: SPCK, 1923), pp. 38–39. See my *House of Wisdom*, p. 98.

13. John 14:22–24 (RSV).

14. Harold W. Attridge and George W. McRae (trans.), *The Gospel of Truth* in James M. Robinson (ed.), *The Nag Hammadi Library* (San Francisco: Harper & Row, 1988), p. 40.

15. Matthew 11:27 (RSV).

16. Matthew 10:29 and Luke 12:6 (RSV).

17. Luke 12:7 (Matthew 10:31) (RSV).

18. See Arundhati Roy's novel, *The God of Small Things* (New York: Random House, 1997), p. 207.

19. Luke 12:31 (Matthew 6:33) (RSV).

20. Mark 1:15 (RSV).

21. Martin Dibelius quoted in Bultmann, *Theology of the New Testament*, vol. 1, p. 32.

22. Matthew 17:1–8; Mark 9:2–8; Luke 9:28–36.

23. Roy, *The God of Small Things*, pp. 205 and 207.

24. Tolkien, *The Lord of the Rings*, p. 292.

25. Mark 4:30–32 (Matthew 13:31–32; Luke 13:18–19).

26. Mark 8:34–35 (RSV) (cf. Matthew 10:38–39; Luke 14:27 and 17:33; John 12:25). "I contend that the content of 'the mystery of the kingdom' in Mark is that the reign or power of God is now manifest in the brokenness of Jesus on the cross, his hiddenness which is to be revealed. Faith in such a Jesus places one 'around him.'" John R. Donahue, *The Gospel in Parable* (Philadelphia: Fortress, 1990), p. 44.

27. Chatwin, *The Songlines*, p. 171.

28. Mark 10:27–30 (RSV). Compare Matthew 19:26–29 and Luke 18:27–30.

29. Roy, *The God of Small Things*, p. 31.

30. Mark 4:26–29.

31. 1 Kings 3:5 and 9 (RSV).

32. Psalm 126:5 (KJ).

33. Tolkien, *Smith of Wooton Major* (Boston: Houghton Mifflin, 1967), p. 38.

34. Wisdom of Solomon 7:11 (NRSV).

35. Tolkien, *Smith of Wooton Major,* p. 38. See his words quoted below on p. 84.

36. 1 Peter 3:11 (KJ).

37. Swami Muktananda, *Getting Rid of What You Haven't Got* (Oakland, Calif.: SYDA Foundation, 1978).

38. Matthew 18:23–35.

39. See above "On Reading," note 34.

40. Matthew 16:16 and 18 (RSV) (cf. Mark 8:27–30 and Luke 9:18–20).

41. Origen, *Prayer* (with *Exhortation to Martyrdom*), trans. John J. O'Meara (New York: Newman, 1954), pp. 15–16.

42. Matthew 19:26; Mark 10:27; Luke 18:27 (RSV).

43. Søren Kierkegaard, *The Sickness unto Death* (with *Fear and Trembling*), trans. Walter Lowrie (Garden City, N.Y.: Doubleday, 1954), pp. 173–74. See my discussion in *The Reasons of the Heart,* pp. 25–31.

44. Hannah Arendt, *The Human Condition* (Chicago: University of Chicago Press, 1958), pp. 236–43.

45. Matthew 13:30 (RSV).

46. Matthew 5:48 and 45 (RSV).

47. G.W. Stonier quoted in *Webster's Third New International Dictionary,* ed. Philip Babcock Gove (Springfield, Mass.: G. & C. Merriam, 1961), p. 1045C (under "heart-whole").

48. Matthew 13:44 (the treasure) and 45–46 (the pearl).

49. These are the titles of Book IV and Book V of Spinoza's *Ethics* in Edwin Curley, ed., *A Spinoza Reader* (Princeton: Princeton University Press, 1994), pp. 197 and 244.

50. Proverbs 15:17 (RSV) and George Colman (1722–1794), *The Clandestine Marriage,* Act 1, scene 2 in E. R. Wood (ed.), *Plays by David Garrick and George Colman the Elder* (Cambridge: Cambridge University Press, 1982), p. 120.

51. Deuteronomy 6:4–5, Matthew 22:37, Mark 12:29–30, Luke 10:27 (RSV).

52. Matthew 24:42 and 25:13, Mark 13:33 and 35, Luke 21:36. Also in the Garden of Gethsemane Matthew 26:38 and 40–41, Mark 14:34 and 37–38 (RSV).

53. Rilke, *Stories of God*, trans. M. D. Herter Norton (New York: Norton, 1963), pp. 115–27, especially p. 126 ("was" and "will be").

54. Heidegger, *Poetry, Language, Thought*, trans. Albert Hofstadter (New York: Harper & Row, 1971), p. 4.

55. Aquinas as quoted by George N. Shuster, *Saint Thomas Aquinas* (New York: Heritage, 1971), p. 3.

56. Broch, *The Death of Virgil*, p. 43.

57. Matthew 26:30 and Mark 14:26 (RSV).

58. Matthew 11:17 and Luke 7:32 (RSV). Cf. the later Parable of the Wicked Husbandmen in Matthew 21:33–46, Mark 12:1–12, and Luke 20:9–19.

59. Matthew 26:29 (RSV) (Mark 14:25 and Luke 22:18).

60. Psalm 117 (my translation). The Hallel is Psalms 113–18 and the second part is Psalms 114–18. See David Daube, *The New Testament and Rabbinic Judaism* (Salem, N.H.: Ayer, rpt. 1984), p. 193.

61. G. R. S. Mead, trans., *The Hymn of Jesus* (London: John M. Watkins, 1963), especially p. 24 (the lines about piping and dancing and wailing and mourning).

62. Psalm 38:9 (RSV).

63. Kafka, *Tagebücher* (New York: Schocken, 1949), p. 475 (May 4, 1915) (my trans.). See my discussion in *The Reasons of the Heart*, p. 5.

64. Nicholas of Cusa (Nicholas Cusanus), *The Vision of God*, trans. Emma Gurney Salter (New York: Ungar, 1969).

65. Matthew 16:23 (KJ). I've used the King James Version here because "savourest" seems closer to the Greek *phroneis* (like the Latin *sapis*) than the modern translations which usually paraphrase, like the Revised Standard Version which has "for you are not on the side of God but of man."

66. Matthew 20:1–16 (the laborers in the vineyard) and 25:14–30 (the talents) (cf. the Parable of the Pounds in Luke 19:11–27).

67. *George MacDonald: An Anthology*, ed. C. S. Lewis (London: Geoffrey Bles, 1946), p. 98 (#255) (from MacDonald's *Unspoken Sermons*).

68. Matthew 7:13–14 and Luke 13:23–24.

69. John 10:7 and 9 (RSV). See my *House of Wisdom*, p. 28.

70. Hammarskjöld, *Markings*, p. 138. See my discussion in *Love's Mind*, p. 21.

71. Saint John of the Cross, *The Dark Night of the Soul*, trans. E. Allison Peers (New York: Doubleday/Image, 1959), p. 35.

72. Luke 23:34 (RSV).

73. The Codex Bezae at Luke 6:4 (my trans.). I am using Erwin Nestle and Kurt Aland, *Novum Testamentum Grace et Latine* (Stuttgart: Württembergische Bibelstalt, 1963), p. 158 (footnote).

74. Luke 11:5–8 (the Friend at Midnight) and 18:1–8 (the Unjust Judge).

75. See my discussion of this saying in *The Peace of the Present*, p. 67.

76. *The Notebooks of Joseph Joubert*, ed. and trans. Paul Auster (San Francisco: North Point, 1983), pp. 180–81 (Maurice Blanchot quoting and commenting on Joubert). See my discussion in *The Music of Time*, p. 15.

77. Luke 7:36–50 (the Sinful Woman/the Two Debtors), 15:3–7 (the Lost Sheep), 15:8–10 (the Lost Coin), 15:11–32 (the Prodigal Son), 18:9–14 (the Pharisee and the Publican). The Lost Sheep is also in Matthew 18:12–14.

78. Chadwick's introduction to Saint Augustine, *Confessions*, p. xxiv.

79. Wendell Berry, *The Wheel* (San Francisco: North Point, 1982), p. 26.

80. Luke 7:47 (RSV).

81. Luke 15:7 and 10 and 32 (RSV).

82. T.S. Eliot, *Four Quartets* (San Diego: Harcourt Brace Jovanovich, 1988), p. 56 ("Little Gidding," lines 166–68). See Julian of Norwich, *Showings*, trans. Edmund Colledge and James Walsh (New York: Paulist, 1974), p. 148 (Short Text: "Sin is necessary") and p. 225 (Long Text: "Sin is necessary, but all will be well, and all will be well, and every kind of thing will be well").

83. Tolkien, *The Lord of the Rings*, p. 292.

84. Luke 10:30 (RSV).

85. Luke 16:9 and 26 (RSV).

86. Luke 14:16 (RSV).

87. Matthew 19:25–26 (RSV).

88. See my discussion of this saying from the Talmud in *The Peace of the Present*, p. 18.

89. Tolkien, *Smith of Wooton Major*, p. 38.

90. Humphrey Carpenter, *Tolkien* (Boston: Houghton Mifflin, 1977), p. 243.

91. Luke 12:19 and 20 (RSV).

92. San Juan de la Cruz, *Poesias Completas*, ed. Cristobal Cuevas (Barcelona: Ediciones B, 1988), p. 89 (my trans.). See Saint John of the Cross, *Collected Works*, p. 416.

93. Luke 5:34–35 (RSV). See Matthew 9:15.

94. Heidegger's preface to William J. Richardson, *Heidegger: Through Phenomenology to Thought* (The Hague: M. Nijhoff, 1963), p. xx. See my discussion in *The Homing Spirit*, p. 17.

95. Dag Hammarskjöld uses this phrase "the way of possibility" in *Markings*, p. 101 (see also pp. 56–58 and p. 12). See my discussion in *The Reasons of the Heart*, p. 28.

96. Mark 14:36 and Luke 1:37 (RSV).

97. Isak Dinesen (= Karen Blixen), *Anecdotes of Destiny* (New York: Random/Vintage, 1985), p. 60. See my discussion in *The Music of Time*, pp. 20–22.

Paradoxes

1. John 3:34 (my translation).

2. Matthew 26:41 and Mark 14:38 (RSV).

3. Mark 14:36, Matthew 26:39, Luke 22:42 (RSV).

4. Matthew 5:1–10.

5. Luke 6:20–23.

6. *The Gospel according to Thomas,* Coptic text ed. and trans. by A. Guillaumont, Henri-Charles Puech, Gilles Quispel, Walter Till, and Yassah 'Abd Al Masih (English text read by Paul S. Minear) (New York: Harper & Row, 1959), p. 25 (#42).

7. Ibid., p. 5 (#7), p. 13 (#18 and #19), and p. 29 (#49).

8. Vincent J. Donovan, *Christianity Rediscovered* (Maryknoll, N.Y.: Orbis, 1982), p. 63.

9. A. C. H. Smith, *The Dark Crystal* (based on the film by Jim Henson) (New York: Holt, Rinehart & Winston, 1982), p. 90.

10. Jean-Pierre de Caussade, *Abandonment to Divine Providence,* trans. John Beevers (New York: Doubleday/Image, 1975).

11. T. S. Eliot, *Four Quartets,* pp. 23 and 32 (the opening and closing lines of "East Coker").

12. Robert A. F. Thurman, *Inside Tibetan Buddhism* (San Francisco: Harper Collins, 1995), p. 17. This is the way Robert Thurman also presented the Four Noble Truths to us in our Buddhist-Christian dialogue mentioned above in the chapter "On Reading," note 13. See my comparison of the Beatitudes and the Four Noble Truths in *The Way of All the Earth*, pp. 50 and 56–57.

13. See my discussion in *The Church of the Poor Devil*, p. 112.

14. See the discussion of "no self" *(anatta)* above pp. 8–9, and see my discussion of "The Sense of I in Christianity" in *Peace of the Present,* pp. 92–101.

15. This is the full title of *The Cloud of Unknowing,* trans. Clifton Wolters (New York: Penguin, 1976), p. 36.

16. Giono, *The Man Who Planted Trees,* p. 51 (in interview with Norma Goodrich).

17. Luke 24:21 (RSV).

18. Tolkien, *The Lord of the Rings,* p. 76.

19. "Everyman" in *Earlier English Drama,* ed. F. J. Tickner (London and Edinburgh: Nelson, 1926), p. 240.

20. Giono, *The Man Who Planted Trees,* p. 50 (in interview with Norma Goodrich).

21. Jung, *Answer to Job,* p. 99.

22. 2 Chronicles 32:31 (RSV). See David Daube's lecture *He That Cometh* (Cowley, Oxford: Church Army Press, 1966), pp. 5–6.

23. See my *Church of the Poor Devil,* p. 17.

24. See Barbara C. Anderson, "Kierkegaard's Despair as a Religious Author" in *International Journal for Philosophy of Religion* (Winter 1973), p. 243.

25. My translation. See my discussion of this saying in *Reasons of the Heart,* p. 92.

Turning Points

1. Polanyi, *The Tacit Dimension,* p. 4.

2. Lull, *The Book of the Lover and the Beloved,* p. 52 (#132) (I have put "one" instead of "he").

3. Gustave Flaubert, *The Temptation of Saint Anthony,* trans. Kitty Mrosovsky (New York: Penguin, 1983).

4. Mark 5:9 (RSV). See Luke 8:30.

5. T. S. Eliot, *The Three Voices of Poetry,* p. 35.

6. See Geoffrey Parrinder, *Jesus in the Qur'an* (Oxford: One World, 1995), pp. 22–29.

7. Robert Bolt, *A Man for All Seasons* (New York: Random House/ Vintage, 1962), p. xiii.

8. Buber, *I and Thou,* pp. 66–67.

9. Buber, *The Way of Response,* ed. N. N. Glatzer (New York: Schocken, 1966), p. 99.

10. Kierkegaard, *Fear and Trembling* (with *Sickness unto Death*), p. 30.

11. Jung, *Answer to Job,* p. 94.

12. John 18:33 and 36, 19:7 and 9 (RSV).

13. Matthew 4:10 and Luke 4:8 (RSV).

14. Kierkegaard, *Sickness unto Death* (with *Fear and Trembling*), p. 147.

15. I am using here "The Harmony of the Gospels" appended to a small New Testament published by Oxford University Press (nd.).

16. David Daube, "He That Cometh" (Cowley, Oxford: Church Army Press, 1966), p. 14. See my discussion in *The Homing Spirit,* p. 20 (and note 34).

17. Tolkien, *The Lord of the Rings,* p. 46.

18. Gerald G. Jampolsky, *Love Is Letting Go of Fear* (New York: Bantam, 1981).

19. Jaroslav Seifert, *Mozart in Prague,* trans. Paul Jagasich and Tom O'Grady (Iowa City: The Spirit That Moves Us Press, 1985), poem #X (no page numbers).

20. Nikos Kazantzakis, *The Odyssey: A Modern Sequel,* trans. Kimon Friar (New York: Simon & Schuster, 1966), p. 673.

21. Erik Erikson, "The Galilean Sayings and the Sense of I," *Yale Review,* Spring 1981, pp. 321–62.

22. Buber, *I and Thou,* p. xv (epigraph from Goethe).

23. Alan Lightman, *Einstein's Dreams* (New York: Pantheon, 1993), p. 52.

24. Mark 6:50 (my trans.) and John 8:58 (RSV).

25. *A Spinoza Reader,* ed. and trans. by Edwin Curley (Princeton: Princeton University Press, 1994), p. 265.

26. A. C. H. Smith, *The Dark Crystal* (New York: Holt, Rinehart & Winston, 1982), p. 90. Quoted above in "Paradoxes," note 9.

27. John 2:24–25 (RSV).

28. John 13:18 (RSV).

29. Matthew 11:25–26 (RSV).

30. Luke 7:47 (RSV).

31. Stephen Spender, *Collected Poems 1928-1985* (New York: Random House, 1986), p. 30 ("The Truly Great").

32. From an unpublished essay by Helen Luke, "Choice in the Lord of the Rings by J. R. R. Tolkien" (Apple Farm Group Discussions, Three Rivers, Mich., n.d.), p. 16 (She gave me permission to use this essay).

33. Max Jacob, *The Dice Cup,* ed. Michael Brownstein (New York: SUN, 1979), p. 5.

34. John 7:27–29 (RSV).

35. See above in "Parables," note 3.

36. John 4:21 (RSV).

37. See my description of the two scenes in *The Homing Spirit,* p. 7 and p. 31.

38. See above in "Parables," note 49.

39. John 8:31–32, 34, 36 (RSV).

40. Simone Weil, *Waiting for God* trans. Emma Craufurd (New York: Harper & Row, 1973), p. 135.

41. *A Spinoza Reader,* pp. 258–64 (Ethics V, ## 29–42) ("under a species of eternity")(I translate "under the aspect of eternity").

42. Meister Eckhart quoted by David Applebaum, *The Vision of Kant* (Rockport, Mass.: Element, 1995), epigraph.

43. Ludwig Wittgenstein, *Tractatus Logico-Philosophicus,* English-German edition, trans. D. F. Pears and B. F. McGuinness (London: Routledge & Kegan Paul, 1961), p. 147 (#6.4311).

44. See, for instance, the discussion of thinking and thanking in "Conversation on a Country Path" in Heidegger, *Discourse on Thinking,* p. 85.

45. Matthew 10:39 (RSV).

46. Roy, *The God of Small Things,* pp. 250, 274, 312.

47. Matthew 5:21–22, 27–28, 33–34, 38–39, 43–44 (RSV).

48. Mark 5:34, 10:52, and Luke 8:48, 17:19 (KJ). I use "made you whole" from KJ deliberately instead of "made you well" of RSV.

49. Hammarskjöld, *Markings,* p. 73 (1952). See my discussion in *The Church of the Poor Devil,* pp. 14–15.

50. Mark 5:28; 10:47 and 48; Luke 17:16 (KJ).

51. Mark 3:5 (KJ).

52. Roland Barthes, *Elements of Semiology,* trans. Annette Lavers and Colin Smith (New York: Hill & Wang, 1968), p. 38. See my discussion in *House of Wisdom,* pp. 81–82.

53. Descartes, *Discourse on Method,* trans. John Veitch in *The Rationalists* (Garden City, N.Y.: Doubleday, 1961), p. 57. See my discus-

sion of the maxim in *The Way of All the Earth*, p. 162 and *The Church of the Poor Devil*, p. 38.

54. Tolstoy, *The Death of Ivan Ilych*, trans. Aylmer Maude (New York: Signet, 1960), p. 156.

55. Wittgenstein, *Tractatus* 6.4311, but here I use Elizabeth Anscombe's translation (New York: Harcourt Brace, 1922). See my discussion in *Time and Myth*, pp. 10–11 and earlier in *The City of the Gods*, pp. 9–10.

56. John 9:4 (KJ). Hammarskjöld, *Markings*, pp. 28, 50, 68, 74, 79, and 126.

57. See my *City of the Gods*, pp. v and 217.

58. John 12:27–28 (RSV).

59. Mark 14:34 and Matthew 26:38 (RSV).

60. Wilhelm Grimm, *Dear Mili*, trans. Ralph Manheim, illus. Maurice Sendak (New York: Farrar, Straus & Giroux, 1988)(pages not numbered).

61. *Grimm's Fairy Tales* (Nine Stories) (New York: Penguin, 1995), p. 1. Lore Segal, *The Juniper Tree and Other Tales from Grimm* (New York: Farrar, Straus & Giroux, 1973), vol.2, p.169 translates simply "In the old days, when wishing still helped. . . ."

62. Alcmaeon, Fragment 2, trans. Kathleen Freeman in *Ancilla to the PreSocratic Philosophers* (Cambridge, Mass.: Harvard University Press, 1957), p. 40. See my discussion in *The Church of the Poor Devil*, p. 23.

63. John 8:28 (my trans.) (RSV has "I am he").

64. Matthew 26:39, Mark 14:36, Luke 22:42 (RSV).

65. *Aboth*, chapter 4, Mishnah 22, trans. J. Israelstam, p. 57 in The Babylonian Talmud, vol. 8, ed. I. Epstein (London: Soncino, 1935). I have put "you" and "your" for "thou" and "thy," etc. Barnett Newman, *The Stations of the Cross* (New York: Guggenheim, 1966), p. 9 has "against thy will. . . ." See my discussion in *House of Wisdom*, p. 88.

66. Luke 22:19 (see also 22:17), Matthew 26:27, Mark 14:23 (RSV).

67. Luke 22:19 (1 Corinthians 11:24) (RSV).

68. Matthew 26:29, Mark 14:25, Luke 22:18 (RSV).

69. Buber, *I and Thou*, p. 67.

70. Matthew 22:15–46, Mark 12:13–37, Luke 20:20–39, and particularly Matthew 22:23–33, Mark 12:18–27, Luke 20:27–39 (the question of the Sadducees on the resurrection) and especially Luke 20:38 (all are alive to God). See my discussion in *The City of the Gods*, pp. 22–24.

71. Ursula LeGuin, *A Fisherman of the Inland Sea* (New York: HarperPrism, 1994), p. 159.

72. Heraclitus, Fragment 18 in Freeman, *Ancilla to the PreSocratic Philosophers*, p. 26.

73. John 20:9 (RSV).

74. Tolkien, *The Lord of the Rings*, p. 988.

75. LeGuin, *A Fisherman of the Inland Sea*, p. 185.

76. W. B. Yeats, *Collected Poems* (New York: Macmillan, 1972), p. 214.

77. Rilke, *Letters to a Young Poet*, trans. M. D. Herter Norton (New York: Norton, 1954), p. 65.

78. John 16:20 (RSV).

Presence

1. Schweitzer, *The Quest of the Historical Jesus*, p. 403.

2. Jane M. Marshall, "He comes to us" (New York: Carl Fischer, 1957) (for chorus of mixed voices with piano or organ).

3. Matthew 28:20 (my trans.).

4. Henryk Sienkiewicz, *Quo Vadis*, trans. Jeremiah Curtin (Boston: Little, Brown, 1919), p. 170.

5. Ephesians 3:17 (KJ).

6. Job 19:25 (RSV) and Luke 20:38 (RSV).

7. John 1:9 (my trans.).

8. See above "On Reading," note 37.

9. See above "Divine Reading," note 31.

10. See above "Divine Reading," note 41.

11. See above "Divine Reading," note 74.

12. See my discussion of this saying in *Peace of the Present*, pp. 99–101.

13. See above "Parables," note 11.

14. See above "Parables," note 37.

15. See above "Parables," note 97.

16. See my discussion of this saying in *Reasons of the Heart*, p. 1.

17. See above "Paradoxes," note 12.

18. See above "Paradoxes," note 24. Kierkegaard makes this distinction in *Fear and Trembling* (See above "On Reading," note 53).

19. See above "Divine Reading," note 76, and "Paradoxes," note 16 and note 20.

20. See above "Divine Reading," note 115.

21. Compare my earlier treatment of the turning points in *A Search for God in Time and Memory*, pp. 8–14, with that above in "Turning Points."

22. See above "On Reading," note 55.

23. David Daube uses the phrase "the test of loneliness" in comparing Jesus and Hezekiah in his lecture "He That Cometh" quoted above in "Turning Points," note 16. The scriptural quotation is about God leaving Hezekiah to himself in 2 Chronicles 32: 31 (RSV). See my discussion in *The Homing Spirit*, pp. 8–18.

24. See above "Turning Points," note 54.

25. See Alexander Nehamas's discussion of this saying of Mann's in *The Art of Living* (Berkeley: University of California, 1998), p. 19.

26. Tolkien, *The Lord of the Rings*, p. 87.

27. See above "Parables," note 71.

28. Marie Sabin, "Women Transformed: The Ending of Mark Is the Beginning of Wisdom" in *Cross Currents*, Summer 1998, pp. 149–68. Here the ending of Mark is taken to be 16:8 as in current scholarship.

29. J. R. R. Tolkien (poems) and Donald Swann (music), *The Road Goes Ever On* (Boston: Houghton Mifflin, 1967).

30. See above "Turning Points," note 43.

INDEX

peace, 15, 37, 42, 89, 92, 93, 96;
as a particular of Jesus' relation
with Abba, 128; as a particular
of the Lord's Prayer, 50, 64,
70, 100, 106; and prayer, 54–55,
64; saying "Yes" to, 121–22;
willingness to do, 14–15
wisdom, 5–6, 68–69, 79; of the
parables, search for,
69–79
Wisdom (Holy Wisdom), 6, 7–8, 9
wisdom sayings, 116
Wise and Foolish Virgins, Parable of
the, 74
withdrawal: following showing in
the Gospels, 65–66; in human
relations, 18, 54, 66; into
solitude as a turning point,
99–109, 119, 136, 137
"with God all things are possible,"
71–72, 83, 87

Wittgenstein, Ludwig, 116, 119, 139
word(s): beyond speech, vii–viii, 14,
16, 124; relationship to music,
30–31
Word, the, vii, 28, 124, 131; becoming
flesh in the Gospel of John,
36–37; and the music, 22–33;
as a person not a doctrine, 17;
spoken by God, 31–32, 131; and
the universality of prologue
to the Gospel of John, 21–22;
variations on theme of as
literary device, 21–22
"world as a bridge," Jesus' saying on,
60, 113–14, 125, 156n3
worlds, many or one, 30–31

Yeats, William Butler, 126
"Yes," saying, 56–58, 121–22, 124,
135–36
"You are my beloved Son," 101–2, 106

JOHN S. DUNNE holds the John A. O'Brien Chair in Theology at the University of Notre Dame. He is the author of many books, including, most recently, *The Mystic Road of Love* (Notre Dame Press, 1999) and *The Music of Time: Words and Music and Spiritual Friendship* (Notre Dame Press, 1996). His *Way of All the Earth* was named by HarperSanFrancisco as one of the hundred best spiritual books of the century.